FROM
INTERN TO VP®

A PROFESSIONAL COACHING SESSION
FOR YOUNG ADULTS

BENECA WARD

WESTBOW
PRESS®
A DIVISION OF THOMAS NELSON
& ZONDERVAN

WestBow Press books may be ordered through booksellers or by contacting:

WestBow Press
A Division of Thomas Nelson & Zondervan
1663 Liberty Drive
Bloomington, IN 47403
www.westbowpress.com
844-714-3454

ISBN: 978-1-6642-9815-6 (sc)
ISBN: 978-1-6642-9814-9 (hc)
ISBN: 978-1-6642-9813-2 (e)

Library of Congress Control Number: 2023907574

Print information available on the last page.

WestBow Press rev. date: 06/14/2023

To young adults a.k.a. industry change makers who are becoming amazing young professionals. I hope the work we do together in this book provides you with an incredibly solid foundation to outline and grow your ideas, visions, and plans forward towards whatever career choice (CEO, Entrepreneur, Artist, Athlete, Doctor etc.) you're interested in and helps you prequalify for your success. I wish you the very best in all you do and hope this book adds a blessing to your life for many years to come!

This book can be utilized as a stand-alone training resource for individual usage and within corporations, universities, organizations, and schools. It can also be licensed as a training and teaching curriculum for group sessions, classes, and other courses. To license the Intern to VP* program, contact scheduling@momentsoffocus.com.

CONTENTS

INTRODUCTION

LET'S GET YOU STARTED

First, this book is for everyone. Whether you are going into a more traditional area of business as an entrepreneur, corporate executive, attorney, engineer, or doctor—a creative area of business as a singer, dancer, artist, or producer—plan to be on the athletic scene as a player, coach, or commentator, have chosen something different or simply don't know what you want to do, this book will help you build your brand in business and in life. Some of the best athletes become the greatest of all time when they are able to combine their skills and capabilities with what they learn from their coach. Most people don't get access to a professional coach until they hit a certain status in their careers. I don't want you to have to wait until then. I created this extensive and personalized professional coaching session for you so that you can take advantage of having a coach now and get ahead in your professional game! I hope you are ready to run because I'm ready to run with you to help you enhance your vision, values, thoughts, and execution for your career development in real time. What if I told you that by the time you finish this book, you will have a clearer perspective about yourself and your next steps? If you answer all the questions I have prepared for you, you will advance in real time more than you can imagine. I want you to envision what it's going to be like once you have your professional objectives, growth strategies, language and script, presence, and more fine-tuned for where you're going. I am going to coach you through and get you ready for the great things that are coming next.

Success has a lot to do with preparation, great decision-making, and being responsible in the areas of your life that you can control. *From Intern to VP®* is a personal, extensive, and tailored professional coaching experience that has guided professionals across the United States to excel in their careers since 2011. It's not enough to just go work *for* a company or sit in a partnership. The sweet spot—in whatever business you go into—is when you learn how to become an amazing professional partner and valued asset to any team you join.

From Intern to VP® has prepared many people to develop mindsets that help them:

- turn their purpose and passion into their profession
- build professional brand names that they're excited about and are significant in their industry of choice
- make their business opportunities (jobs, partnerships, meetings, interviews, internships, and volunteerism) work for them
- create the lives they want

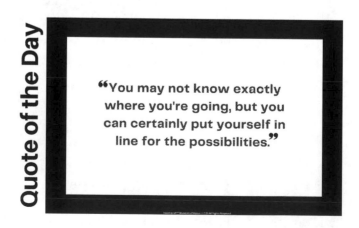

Quote of the Day

"You may not know exactly where you're going, but you can certainly put yourself in line for the possibilities."

We don't always know where the opportunities that we're presented with will lead us, but when we align ourselves with those who have the potential to connect us to our dreams, we typically gain something great and unexpected. You will grow through this process, and I am going to give you everything I can within the pages of this book. Whether you are reading this because your company gave it to you as a part of your training and orientation, you're looking to make moves on your own, or you received it from your school, this book will help you advance your perspective and professional life. Congratulations on taking control in this next step towards your success! It will give you an advantage and provide you with a mentality that will be useful throughout your career. In the future, the question will not be "Will I be given opportunities?" Instead, it will be "Have I taken the time to determine what the right opportunities are for me?" and "Have I prequalified myself for them?"

Whenever you're working with anyone, you should know a bit about who they are so that you know how and why you should gain insight from them. Since I'm going to be your coach through this part of your professional and leadership development, I'd like to take a moment to introduce myself. As an executive advisor, an international speaker, an author, and a producer, I work with Fortune 100/500 companies, entrepreneurs, professional athletes, TV and film directors, young professionals, and more. During this process, I'll be here to work with you one-on-one. I'm excited to help you excel in the specific career or industry of your choice and build a substantial professional brand name. I am working with you because I know that, with guidance, you can push through to your defined level of success.

Prepare to highlight the tips, tools, and strategies that I have outlined for you in this book. Everything I ask and share with you is about and is for you. Get your mind ready to fill these pages with your goals, visions, and thoughts so that you can create action plans that move your life forward in real time.

I started my career in high school, and I know what it's like to be young and have a desire to do great things while needing support and direction. I know what it's like to have a vision and an interest in contributing to the world in more than one area of business. I went from being a sixteen-year-old intern in Hollywood to becoming a television executive, which is where

I worked for twenty years. While I was there, my interest in writing led me to write my first book, which prompted an invitation to the White House.

I took key principles from that book and developed the Intern to VP° program so that young adults like you would have the knowledge and support to focus on:

- who you are
- who you want to become
- how to draw a map to where you want to go
- what you plan to do and how you plan to lead when you arrive

I was blessed to learn a lot along the way up, but if I had been given all the knowledge, insight, and direction in this book going into my career, I would have taken larger steps and moved forward on a different level.

I do not want to guide you onto anyone else's pathway; instead, I want to coach you to strategically grow and excel on your journey. Every page that you turn to will have a reminder, a tip, or a strategy. Every question has been developed to take you to your next answer. Together, we are going to enhance your vision for your future based on who you are today and where you want to go next. When working with CEOs and entrepreneurs, I often help them develop what I call their *Executive Scripts*. I help them develop the answers, questions, and statements they want to provide to others based on the intentions of their vision. I'll help you with this with the *professional scripting* assistance I have included for you.

Every question has been intentionally designed to help you:

- discover and articulate your thoughts and intentions
- develop your professional scripts
- design your life's road map

The professional scripting assistance is a priceless part of our work together, but the only way this gift will be worth anything to you is if you activate it by answering every question openly and honestly. If you don't have an answer right away, it's okay. However, make sure you stop and find the answer by researching, interviewing others, or reflecting about how you really feel. You should not be pushed into a specific career path; instead, you should be guided in how to investigate which long-term career choices will work best for you based on certain aspects of who you are. Our work together is intended to help you figure out, determine, and announce who you are and where you want to go. This will help you get to where you're meant to be and will serve as an asset for those who are willing to give you an opportunity to work with them. I'll assist as a driver to get you to your next steps, but your answers will create the road map for where we're going. The questions I ask you today will be asked repeatedly by other people at different levels of your career. Having your answers ready now will help you when you get to where you're going.

There's one more thing before we get started. There might be concepts that you have heard before. I tell my clients that you may have gone to the gas station to fill up in the past, but I'm going to show you how to use this fuel to go somewhere different.

In *From Intern to VP*®, I am going to take you through a professional brand and leadership development program based on ten keys of brand development. We're going to work together to help you:

- discover your brand
- set your expectations
- develop your brand name
- prepare for future opportunities
- create a road map for your career
- learn how to network effectively
- form strategic partnerships
- become business savvy
- successfully launch your brand on social media
- develop your organization affiliations

One of the first lessons in leadership development is understanding that the first person you're ever going to truly lead is yourself. Once people start to see your personal accomplishments, they will begin to ask about the details surrounding your success—and they might even ask you to lead others. Our coaching session will be a workshop that you will be leading yourself through with my help.

Let's start by developing your professional script. Answer the following questions while keeping in mind that each answer will serve as a building block for the next one. Eventually, all your answers will become key statements in how you represent yourself or your brand name on a regular basis. Remember to prepare your answers in complete sentences that you will be comfortable giving in a meeting, in an interview, or from a podium. Since these questions will be asked continuously throughout your career, be prepared to write them down and edit them as you grow. You can't edit what you don't write. Don't let your fear of writing the "perfect" answers prevent you from writing down your initial thoughts because your thoughts, with editing, will evolve into your plans.

Who are you? It is important to identify and remember who you are when making decisions. Get into the habit of identifying who you are and knowing the answers to the questions about your life. How would you describe your personality? What are your personal interests and desires? This assessment will help you determine what type of atmosphere you really want to work in and realize what you need to add to your life outside of work to feel balanced.

I am someone who loves and dislikes:

_____

_____

_____

_____

_____

_____

_____

_____

_____

_____

I am someone who is motivated by:

_____

_____

_____

_____

_____

_____

_____

_____

What do you want to help contribute to this world? Some people are here to write songs, jokes, or TV shows that help others tap into their emotions and feel better, some people are here to research and find ways to heal diseases, and some people are here to build airplanes that allow people to travel. What do you feel led to be a part of? You may have more than one answer.

_____

_____

_____

_____

_____

_____

_____

_____

_____

I would like to contribute:

_____

_____

_____

_____

_____

_____

_____

_____

_____

What brings you joy to be a part of? If money didn't matter, what professional position would make you excited to be a part of daily and why?

If money didn't matter, professionally I would:

_____

_____

_____

_____

_____

_____

_____

_____

_____

It brings me joy to be a part of:

_____

_____

_____

_____

_____

_____

_____

Not all people use maps to develop their careers. Some people just go with the flow or follow opportunities as they come. We, however, are going to consider the benefits of mapping out your career so that, as you move forward, you'll know what to look for, ask for, and apply for based on your interests and possibilities. Although the directions in your career map may change as you gain exposure to new things and develop new interests, the roads you travel should always be aligned with who you are. Therefore, you need to be organized in your thoughts and actions as you head toward your destination. Some career maps can be more challenging to develop than others based on what you're planning to accomplish. After researching what it will take, are you willing to commit to the path toward your greatness? If so, what temporary costs are you willing to pay? What sacrifices are you willing to make? Are you willing to sacrifice time with friends or not making a lot of money while you are preparing for your next step?

Understanding that all things are possible, I am willing to do the following to prepare for my goals:

_____

_____

_____

_____

_____

_____

_____

_____

_____

Working in *any* career is about service. The following chart includes several of the options to choose from.

First, notice that each profession has a client and a service affiliated with it. Then, answer the questions below.

These questions are not meant to simply help you find the perfect "job." They're more about identifying the type of work you want to spend your life's time in. Time is like money. How and where you spend it matters. You get twenty-four hours per day to invest in something. I am going to help you spend your time investing in your current, future, and legacy plans. Just because you choose one career now, it doesn't mean that you can't expand into something else in the future.

We'll talk about how to expand your plans when we discuss your professional vision later. However, to start, I want you to take a moment to think through your answers. To work on building your brand name, or what everyone thinks about when mentioning your name, we must first make sure that what we build is true to you. Therefore, I don't want you to rush through your thoughts. Take a moment to envision and get excited about what your life will look like when you are able to maneuver around in the life plan that you want to live through.

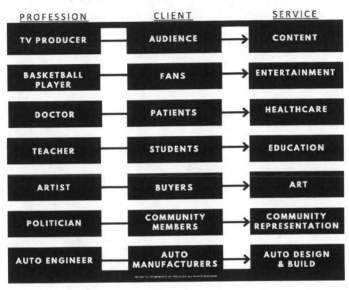

Professional

CLIENT SERVICE CHART

PROFESSION	CLIENT	SERVICE
TV PRODUCER	AUDIENCE	CONTENT
BASKETBALL PLAYER	FANS	ENTERTAINMENT
DOCTOR	PATIENTS	HEALTHCARE
TEACHER	STUDENTS	EDUCATION
ARTIST	BUYERS	ART
POLITICIAN	COMMUNITY MEMBERS	COMMUNITY REPRESENTATION
AUTO ENGINEER	AUTO MANUFACTURERS	AUTO DESIGN & BUILD

What and/or how are you most interested in serving others?

My goal is to serve others by:

_____

_____

_____

_____

_____

_____

_____

_____

_____

_____

Why does serving in this way interest you?

I am interested in this area of service because:

_____

_____

_____

_____

_____

_____

_____

_____

_____

What profession(s) does/did this lead you to pursue? Who is your perfect client or customer?

This has led me to pursue:

_____

_____

_____

_____

_____

_____

_____

_____

_____

My perfect client and/or customer is:

_____

_____

_____

_____

_____

_____

_____

_____

Now let's move forward. Success in our sessions will be determined by your 100 percent participation:

- Take life-changing notes!
- Apply what you're assessing to your life instantly.
- Stay engaged in your progress.
- Commit to leaving this coaching session in a state of active growth and development.
- Listen, learn, question, implement, and teach.

Tip: Sharing what you learn in this book with your friends, family, and coworkers can help you retain the information and can give you an opportunity to practice your leadership skills.

Prepare to Develop in Real Time

- "Life is a class, and your salary is the tuition for your life." Any job you take should provide you with "credits" or "benefits" for career advancement so that you can graduate to the next level of development. Credits could be exposure, experience, or leadership skills. Benefits could be being paid to learn or having opportunities to contribute to and serve in an industry of your choice.

- Develop a professional syllabus for your advancement. Because this is an accelerated coaching program, you will be utilizing much of what we cover at different stages of your life. Don't feel like you need to use everything you learn right now. Throughout this process, I'm going to help you create a personalized syllabus to outline what you need to learn for your career development, solely based on your vision for your future. This will allow you to look for opportunities to gain "credits" so that you can graduate to your next level.
- Identify the purpose of your passion. Your story and the reasons why you're doing something matter. It can connect people to you and drive them to wanting to help you move forward. Having the ability to answer the following questions can determine whether you will be invited to discuss future opportunities.

Beyond your general interests, why do you want to do what you're so passionate about? What drives you in this direction?

The driving factor behind my why is:

_____

_____

_____

_____

_____

_____

_____

_____

_____

Establish a baseline for your next level of development and leadership. What does the next level of leadership look like for you?

My next level of leadership involves (next steps, desires, and plans):

_____

_____

_____

_____

_____

_____

_____

_____

_____

Build a professional brand name for yourself that is recognized for its greatness by the people, companies, and organizations you want to partner with. It's important to build a professional brand that other people want to be connected to and invest in. As you're starting to figure out where you want to be with your work, also consider:

- who you want to work with
- why they would want to work with you based on who you are, what you're doing, and/or how you can work together

Tip: You're not going to be doing business with everyone. Although it's great to have a broad network, it's essential to develop a strategic group of business contacts who are unique to your area of business and will support, guide, and help you grow your vision.

Create professional scripts that help you communicate with others as you move to the next level. Successful conversations in business don't just happen. The answers are strategically developed long before the questions are asked—based on experience, exposure, research, and anticipation. The ability to have a great conversation has a lot to do with being able to execute well-developed thoughts that are just waiting for the right question to bring them out. Your answers in this book will become your professional script. You will be able to use these answers at work events, interviews, meetings, and dinner parties—and you'll be grateful that you did the work today so that you don't stumble with your answers later.

Become fluent in the business of being you. At the end of your coaching session, you'll be more aware and in a better position to articulate your thoughts about who you are, you'll be more confident about where you're going, and you'll have a clearer vision of how to get there.

LEADERSHIP HAPPENS AT EVERY LEVEL

CEOs and politicians are not the only types of leaders. You're expected to have the ability to lead from wherever you stand, recognize your leadership skills, and know what you can add to a team based on your experience. Other people don't determine whether you're a leader. Your skill sets, traits, and actions determine your leadership status.

Leadership development starts with understanding:

- who you are today
- who you'd like to become or how you'd like to maintain in your current position
- your intentions behind your plans
- what to pack and how to prepare for your journey
- your professional leadership plans

Many young professionals don't take the time to acknowledge their abilities or research what they will need to know for their next opportunity until the opportunity has already presented itself. Unfortunately, that is often too late.

Identify five core strengths that make you an asset to a team. Examples include:

- self-development or team development
- strategic thinking
- project management

Identify five growth spots that you have been told you need to develop:

- presentation skills
- being afraid to ask for help
- avoiding difficult conversations
- being insensitive to others
- having an "I know" attitude

Identifying these strengths and growth spots will help you to acknowledge, develop, and make any necessary adjustments to these areas at a faster rate.

Core Strengths   Growth Spots

1.	1.
2.	2.
3.	3.
4.	4.
5.	5.

Stay focused on your big goals and remember that life is a class and every opportunity (job, meeting, or event) will help you graduate. Whatever you've identified in this chart will be listed on your professional syllabus as something to strengthen or maintain. Since every opportunity provides credits or benefits, you should be looking for jobs, activities, and events that will prepare you for what's next.

Make sure you keep a proper perspective of who and what you have access to while considering what you're looking for and where you're going. If one of your growth spots has to do with enhancing your communication skills, look for opportunities that will give you a chance to practice growing in that area. For instance, when your employer is looking for a volunteer to give a presentation, even if you're not getting paid for it in cash, remember that it could help you gain credits toward your advancement.

As for your strengths, look for projects that will enhance them. This can move you to the next level of leadership in these core areas. Since no one grows without the watering of others, seek help from other professionals, mentors, and human resource representatives. If the only resource you have access to is the internet, don't be afraid to use it to find the knowledge you need.

Not everyone on the internet is an expert, but there are thousands of experts online. If you need clarity and do not have access to a person who can help, the easiest thing to do is go online and find a reputable company or a qualified individual who posts tips, tools, and strategies that can provide you with insight.

Look for organizations that specialize in your areas of interests since they often post free insights that can help you grow. We'll discuss the importance of organization affiliations and engagement later.

Now that we've gotten started, let's prepare to focus on our next section: "Building Your Brand." First, identify your key takeaways from this section so that you can build on what you have acknowledged and move forward more effectively.

KEY TAKEAWAYS

My key takeaways that I will move into a state of action are:

_____

_____

_____

_____

_____

_____

_____

_____

_____

_____

_____

_____

_____

_____

_____

_____

_____

_____

_____

_____

_____

_____

PART I

DISCOVERING YOUR BRAND

Branding is creating a name or something specific for a product or person that sets it totally apart from others. Professional and career brand development is an intentional and proactive way to decide how you'll be perceived as a professional in your industry. In this part of our session, my goal is for you to discover your professional brand, identify what will differentiate you from others, and set a reputation that makes other people want to invite you to go everywhere *you* want to go.

Tip: Always identify the values in your personal brand before you build your professional brand. If integrity, loyalty, trust, and justice are true to your personal brand, they will also be a reflection of what your team can expect from you, and once you are a leader, what you will expect from them.

BRAND-BUILDING WORDS

Intentional: It is essential to be intentional about everything that you do from this point on as you build your brand. Take every action and have every conversation with a plan in mind of how it will fit into the purpose of what you have designed for your life. Whether it's about work or your life with friends and family, question what you're about to say or participate in before you do it. Ask yourself, "Does this fit into the future I have outlined for myself? Does this fit into my brand?" Make sure you think everything through beyond the effects that it will have on your life today or this month. The people who take big steps forward typically strategize, think every step through, and stay in line with their steps.

Consistent: Consistency builds brands. Whatever you do repeatedly is what you become known for. It's that simple. By the time you are in elementary school, your teachers have built a brand name about you, and they write reports based on your behavior and work habits. Some kids are branded as the "quiet girl" or the "overenergized boy." It is impossible to not have a brand name or reputation when you are around people. The difference between then and now is that now you have an opportunity to intentionally rebrand yourself, create action plans that move you forward, and become who you really want to be based on the vision that you foresee for your life.

What brand names of cars, sports teams, technology, or food companies are your favorites, what are they best known for, and why do people invest in them?

_____

_____

_____

_____

_____

_____

_____

_____

_____

Thinking back to your reputation as an employee or student, as it pertains to your work, what are you best known for?

Regarding my work, I am best known for:

_____

_____

_____

_____

_____

_____

_____

_____

_____

Why do (or should) employers, friends, or family members invest their time, money, or opportunities in you?

I am a good investment because I am someone who: (for example: will turn their time, money, or opportunities into ...)

_____

_____

_____

_____

_____

_____

_____

_____

What differentiates you from other young professionals? Is it your vision, leadership skills, communication style, desire to apply what you learn, determination, personal drive, pleasant personality, or ability to work with or motivate others?

What makes me unique in contrast to other young professionals is:

Is what you're best known for, as it pertains to your work ethic, what you want to be known for? If not, what do you want to add to who you are?

In the long term, I really want to be known for being someone who:

_____

_____

_____

_____

_____

I also want to be known as someone who has been able to accomplish:

_____

_____

_____

_____

_____

_____

_____

_____

_____

ELEMENTS OF BRAND DEVELOPMENT

Most brands focus on their products and the company benefits associated with creating or providing those products. They pay particular attention to:

- the product's development
- how they foresee it being utilized
- how it will be identified
- the level of its quality
- the value it adds to the consumer
- the benefits that the company gains from their efforts

- its positioning in the market
- its marketing and advertising plan

Your professional brand development is very similar in structure, but you are the product. Now, we're going to outline who you are from your perspective using the chart below, but first let's talk about your favorite brands. Focusing on them should help with your clarity as we start focusing on you.

What are your two favorite brands?

_____

_____

_____

_____

_____

_____

_____

_____

_____

_____

The brand names that you admire have all taken the time to build out their legacy plans and have set an example for others to follow. I always tell my clients that if you're not leaving a legacy, you're just leaving.

What impact are you planning to have in your industry, and what legacy are you planning to leave?

The impact I plan to have in my industry is one that:

_____

_____

_____

_____

_____

_____

_____

_____

_____

As it pertains to my legacy, I want people to be able to say: (for example: that I developed, contributed, or created change by …)

_____

_____

_____

_____

_____

_____

_____

_____

_____

_____

Pick one of your favorite brands and describe the vision they have set for the company. What did they want it to become—and how can you tell?

_____

_____

_____

_____

_____

_____

_____

_____

_____

Tip: Some of the questions in this book may sound similar. That's intentional. In the future, people will ask the same questions in different ways to confirm your understanding of a situation—or the question may be used in a different context. It is up to you to train your mind to listen to conversations with a keen ear.

As we go through this process—and you begin to read and evaluate your thoughts about who you are and what your plans are for moving forward—your outlook will change. Your answers may begin to adjust to the new you that you are developing. As your answers change, you'll be able to see your growth.

Corporations spend endless hours deciding what their product will be before it is released to the world. I want you to tell me who you are preparing the world to know you as. Your answers will provide direction for the next step on your career road map.

THE PRODUCT (YOU)

Who are you preparing yourself to become? (Don't be shy or limiting.)

I am preparing myself to become:

_____

_____

_____

_____

_____

_____

_____

_____

_____

Next, think about which areas (education, skills, and specific job experience) you need to develop as a professional to reach your career goals.

_____

_____

_____

_____

_____

_____

_____

_____

_____

Tip: Self-awareness is a leadership trait, and self-assessment is a leadership skill that lets people know that you are not just paying attention to what you want and what you'll need to do to accomplish your goals but you're also very mindful of who you truly are as an individual and what you have to add to the world. How you lead yourself is always going to be a reflection on your abilities to lead others. Furthermore, people are more likely to help you when they don't feel like they have to carry you into every step forward but can guide you as you walk on your own.

Coaches like to work with athletes who are excited about their sport, come ready to run, work out on their own, are willing to listen, and take their direction to the next level. Mentors and other professionals who are open to help you are very similar. The more prep work or personal discovery and development you've done before you meet with someone who can help you, the further and faster they can take you. This is why the work you are doing now is so valuable.

People who can help you are great assets, and you never want to waste your resources. Some people, however, will only talk to you when they feel that you're ready or prequalified for their level of advice. So, get ready. People who like you or have closer relationships with you will often help you regardless. Still, they will only be able to help you at the level that you have expressed and/or displayed that you're at. If you come into a conversation at a kindergarten level, just knowing your name and a little bit about what you like and are interested in, that is what they will talk to you about. But if you come in at a professional level where you can express the following concepts, it will make it easier to guide you to your next level:

- what you want your name to represent
- what you're interested in
- how you'd like to move forward in your life
- what positions you'd like to move into

Sometimes people don't get the best out of their mentoring opportunities because they have not been fully transparent about their vision.

As a professional, I need to develop my:

_____

_____

_____

_____

_____

_____

_____

_____

_____

Tips: When developing your career goals, always prepare a full gap analysis (or outline) that shows you what sits in the gap that you need to accomplish like job experience, education, industry knowledge, etc., between where you are today and where you plan to be. The following are quick steps:

- Acknowledge your ultimate goals.
- Recognize where you currently are in your position, experience, and so forth and then outline each step that it will take to meet your goals.
- Identify what your next step should be based on your analysis. Whether it is applying for a specific job, taking a management position, or joining a professional organization, set it as an official goal.
- Next, research, examine, and make a checklist of the requirements necessary to meet that goal. Your checklist will become a part of your career road map. Check off any requirements on your list that you already meet and circle any that you don't. What you have circled will become your immediate targets. For instance, if a leadership position you would like to apply for requires a specific certification or degree that you do not have, circle it.
- Research and develop an action plan and timeline for how you can meet any requirements you're missing so that you prequalify

yourself to be in position to accomplish each small goal that leads to your ultimate plans.

VISION

How do you intend for your skills and talents to be utilized as a professional in your industry?

In my industry, I intend that my skills and talent will be utilized in, by, or through:

_____

_____

_____

_____

_____

_____

_____

_____

_____

IDENTITY

What do you want people to associate your first and last name or brand name with when it is mentioned in your industry?

When my name is mentioned in my industry, I want people to associate it with:

_____

_____

_____

_____

_____

_____

_____

_____

_____

_____

QUALITY

What level of quality do you want to be associated with your brand? What are you looking to invest into your brand name (through your time, money, additional classes and programs, and whatever physical investment it may require like showing up to events or working late)? Please share the details on what your investment will look like moving forward.

I want my brand name to be known for a _____ (mid, high or average) level of quality. The investment I am willing to make is one that requires that I:

_____

_____

_____

_____

_____

_____

_____

_____

BENEFITS

What benefits do you gain from being who you are currently? What benefits will you gain once you accomplish your professional goals? Every successful company takes in some sort of benefit. It's important that you identify what you're gaining from what you're developing so that when times are tough, you remember the benefit and why you're doing what you're doing. Oftentimes, the benefit will be for you, but sometimes the benefit will be for others. Either way, it's important to acknowledge this now because it will become like gasoline in your tank when you are working hard and feel like you are on empty.

These are not meant to be bragging rights; instead, they are meant to help you evaluate what your faith, determination, and efforts have helped you accomplish.

Being who I am now has allowed me to (for example: secure great job opportunities, meet with, participate in, or have access to):

_____

_____

_____

_____

_____

_____

_____

_____

_____

_____

Once I accomplish my professional goals, I expect that the benefits I will gain or have access to will be:

_____

_____

_____

_____

_____

_____

_____

_____

_____

VALUE

What benefits do other people gain from having you on their team or in their network? What value would you like to be known for bringing to others?

It is beneficial to have me on a team because I can help with:

_____

_____

_____

_____

_____

_____

_____

_____

_____

I am valuable because I can add a unique:

_____

_____

_____

_____

_____

_____

_____

_____

_____

YOUR POSITION

How are you planning to position yourself in the market of your industry among other professionals? What do you want your positioning differentiator to be?

I am planning to position myself in my industry as someone who:

_____

_____

_____

_____

_____

_____

_____

_____

_____

MARKETING (YOUR COMMUNICATION)

How do you plan to market your abilities so that people will know you are available to serve and participate at the level you have planned? Have you considered what your advertising plan will be beyond social media?

I plan to market my abilities by:

_____

_____

_____

_____

_____

_____

_____

_____

_____

_____

Tip: People often think that branding and marketing are the same, but they are not. The easiest way to think about it is to think of branding as creating and marketing as advertising. You build a brand and then send it out to the market for others to examine and decide if they want to invest in or partner with it.

Companies spend countless hours developing, researching, and adjusting their brands before they spend time and money advertising its official launch. You should never produce commercials for a brand that is not developed at a level that will allow it to sustain in its market. It's better to delay a launch (on social media, at live events, and at conferences) than to introduce yourself to your industry before you've developed the basics (your vision, intent, and mission) of your brand. Take the time to set a solid foundation that your audience can buy into and believe in.

Before you spend time and money advertising who you are on social media or investing in tickets for events where you'll be able to network with the who's who in your industry, develop your brand so that what you are advertising is solid and true.

Most people will not give you the time or space in their minds to prove that you're different than you were the first time they met you.

CONFIDENCE AND HUMILITY

Confidence and humility go hand in hand. You must be confident enough to know who you are and what you know, humble enough to acknowledge and learn what you don't know, and smart enough to know the difference.

- Are you confident enough to articulate what you know, humble enough to express what you don't, and smart enough to know the difference?
- Do you have enough confidence and courage to stand next to other people as they advertise who you are in their meetings and conversations?
- Are you humble enough to know that as a leader in a world that is forever changing, you will always need to grow, learn, and develop?

MAKE OPPORTUNITIES WORK FOR YOU

Whether you're entering or settling into a new business, job, internship, or volunteer opportunity—or are preparing for an important meeting—making these opportunities work for your benefit has a lot to do with your ability to develop great partnerships with companies and people who are a good fit for your brand, goals, and career plans. Think about the company you are working with now—or the one that you plan to work with—when answering the following questions.

Examining Your Partnership

 **INTENTION**

 **CONTRIBUTIONS**

 **PLANS**

OPPORTUNITIES

 **EXPECTATIONS**

Intern to VP Mastermind of Focus LLC, All Rights Reserved

INTENTION

What is your intention behind your partnership? What do you intend to happen during and after your process there?

My intention behind partnering with my company is that I will be able to:

_____

_____

_____

_____

_____

_____

_____

_____

_____

_____

PLANS

What are your exact plans for your process? Feel free to outline different scenarios. "If this happens, I plan to _____, but if I take this track, I look to _____."

The plans that I have drawn out for this partnership include:

_____

_____

_____

_____

_____

_____

_____

_____

_____

EXPECTATIONS

What are your expectations? What do you expect will happen for and because of you?

Through my work here, I expect that:

_____

_____

_____

_____

_____

_____

_____

_____

_____

_____

I believe that the following will happen for me:

_____

_____

_____

_____

_____

_____

_____

CONTRIBUTIONS

What contributions do you foresee making to the organization? How do you expect the organization to contribute to your growth?

These are the contributions I foresee making to the organization:

_____

_____

_____

_____

_____

_____

_____

_____

_____

I expect the organization will contribute to my growth by:

_____

_____

_____

_____

_____

_____

_____

_____

_____

_____

What additional opportunities could come from your partnership?

I imagine having the opportunity to (for example, meet with or be mentored by company executives, join employee resource groups/organizations, be promoted, sit on committees):

_____

_____

_____

_____

_____

_____

_____

_____

_____

_____

THE SUPERPOWER IN EFFECTIVE COMMUNICATION AND PRESENTATIONS

It's important to become extremely intentional about what you are communicating to others. Communication is simply a way of sending a message. Every time you are around others, you are communicating. Whether it is with your body language or your words, you are always sending a message.

Sometimes you may be quiet, but your body language and face expressions send a loud message that says:

- Hey, come talk to me.
- Please don't come over here and talk to me.

You may walk into an office and your body language tells others that:

- You are confident and prepared.
- You are insecure and nervous.

The word *presentation* has become very formal. Many people think a presentation is an official process that requires standing in front of a large audience, presenting facts, and answering questions. The truth is that whenever you are around others, you are presenting. Every conversation is a presentation of thought. You are presenting parts of who you are and what you represent. Effective communication, through conversation, has a purpose, a requirement, a communication style, and an intended effect.

The purpose of communicating verbally is using words to make actions happen. From here on out, I want you to upgrade your conversations, making sure they all have a purpose. The intent should be to express or gain information and knowledge for a specific reason. Regardless of what the subject matter is, the point is to train your mind to be clear about the purpose of any conversation you are giving your time to. This will help you understand what you can gain from it and how you can contribute to it:

- There's a superpower in the ability to communicate effectively and give a presentation or present a solid thought from wherever you're standing and to whomever you're talking to.
- Whether your words are moving work forward, changing someone's emotional status, or creating a new atmosphere for others, they should be intentional and carry the power of an action. Many people contribute to conversations without proper thought or intention. They talk just to be talking or to be included in a conversation.
- Remember that whatever you do helps build your reputation. If you become known as someone who talks just to be heard or someone who adds empty words to conversations rather than as a thought leader, you will not be invited to meetings or teams to help make important decisions.
- Many people think you are only brought in to be a thought leader once you've been promoted to a leadership position. However, you can be promoted to a leadership position once people see you as a thought leader.

EVERY TIME YOU COMMUNICATE, YOU'RE PRESENTING.

Think: Casual, Conference Room and Media

THE PURPOSE	THE REQUIREMENTS
• Use words to get results • Express or gain information/knowledge for a specific purpose	• Insight • Foresight • Vision • Knowledge • Expectation (Heightened Conversations?)
THE HOW	**THE EFFECT**

• Communication/Presentation Style:
  ○ Direct/Blunt/Achievement Focused/People Oriented (Emotional Intelligence in Progress?)
 	
• Language Variations
  ○ Peer to Peer/ Upper Executives/ Clients / Staff / Customers
 	
• Leadership Style:
  ○ Directive/Authoritative/ Affiliative/ Participative/ Coaching
	Impact on your next steps, team, work and partnerships (Your words are weighted, and they count.)

In an effective conversation, you gain or provide insight, foresight, vision, knowledge, and/or expectations about something specific. It may sound like a no-brainer, but you'd be surprised how many people walk away from discussions that don't include these elements feeling like they just had an empty exchange with the person they were talking to.

Effective conversations contain certain characteristics:

- Insight is the ability to have a clear deep understanding of a situation. This requires you to contribute to conversations and/or ask questions on a deeper level.
- Foresight is the ability to judge what may happen in the future and requires consideration of the long-term effects of decisions.
- Vision is something you should walk into every conversation with, when possible. You want to have or quickly develop an idea of how the discussion may go based on the topic, who's in the room, and what you may be able to add.
- Knowledge is a staple that you should look to receive or provide in every conversation. There could be discussions that you'll walk into and have no idea how you can add to them.
- If you find yourself in a place and you don't know what to say, don't say anything—just listen. You don't always have to contribute.
- If you're asked to contribute, and you don't have an answer, be honest. You can always respond with something firm like, "I am not familiar with that, please share more" or "I don't know, but I am happy to look into it right away."
- It's better to be known as someone who is confident about what they know, transparent about what they don't, and able to quickly find resources to supplement their lack of knowledge rather than someone who is a "temporary talker" and not a reliable source of facts. A temporary talker is someone who provides whatever information they feel will get them through the conversation in that moment. Oftentimes, however, it's not useful for the team in the long run.
- The words "I don't know" can be strong, honest, and freeing. If you are going to a work meeting, you should have a plan going in.

Research as much as you can to get an agenda, find out as much as you can about the topic, and determine if there are any deliverables you may be expected to bring to the conversation.

- Expectations are a basic part of communication. Everyone expects something when you enter a conversation.
- As it pertains to your brand, do people expect that you will heighten the discussions you are involved in?
- Are you known as someone who knows how to pull back when it's not necessary for you to answer all the questions?
- Would people say that you know how to read the audience that you're speaking to? Do you know what you should and should not say based on who you're talking to?

When I'm invited into a conversation, people expect that:

_____

_____

_____

_____

_____

_____

_____

_____

The How: Your communication style, your ability to be flexible in your language, and your leadership style have a lot to do with how effective your message will be.

- Communication/Presentation Style: By nature, is your communication style direct, blunt, achievement focused, people oriented, full of emotional intelligence, or all the above at different times based on the conversation and circumstances at hand? Your presentation style will often be based on your personality or job title. However, you should be able to be flexible and adjust based on the nature of the conversation and/or who you're speaking with.

My natural communication style is:

_____

_____

_____

_____

_____

_____

_____

_____

_____

_____

LANGUAGE VARIATIONS

Family members, peers, senior-level executives, clients, staff, and customers all require different types of language. Do you know how to be flexible in your language style depending on who you're talking to? Code switching used to refer to when people would switch from two or more languages based on context. Over time, it became a broader term. For the sake of this exercise, let's focus on the benefits of being able to code switch in a business environment.

You're most effective when you can speak the language of the person you're talking to. When speaking with executives, the terms you use will often be those that relate to their work and culture. Those same terms may not be those that you would use when speaking with your customers, colleagues, friends, or family.

The type of audience I need to learn how to speak to is (clients, executives, or peers):

_____

_____

_____

_____

_____

_____

_____

_____

As you excel in your career, you will be given the opportunity to work with people and lead projects. Paying attention to and developing your communication style now—making it what you want it to become—is crucial. Your communication style determines how you speak, act, and react in various situations, and how people will describe how you interact, get along with, or relate to others.

Some people have a tendency to come across as very direct or blunt. In some circumstances, being direct can be beneficial, but in other circumstances, it is not. There are others who are extremely soft-spoken. That can work well in a work environment—or not. My goal is to make sure you are familiar with four of the most common communication styles so that you can study them and recognize how they can affect your ability to share your messages effectively in a professional setting.

COMMON COMMUNICATION STYLES

PASSIVE

People who have a passive communication style are typically quiet. They don't like to be seen or make direct eye contact, and they act indifferently about most things. Nothing really seems to bother them or drive them to take charge. They usually go with the flow. Although being easy-going can be a wonderful character trait, it can sometimes be seen in the workplace as an inability—or lack of desire—to make important decisions.

If you are passive by nature, consider how your communication style will affect your ability to do well in your position and your professional brand. Being passive might be a great fit for the position you want. However, if it is not, consider what you can do to break out of your shell. Take small steps like intentionally not providing "yes" or "no" answers. Look for opportunities to add to conversations. Take speech classes. Research to be certain that what you are adding to a conversation is correct, write down your thoughts, and then insert your point of view with confidence. Look for small group projects at work or in your community that encourage you to grow in your communication skills so that you practice asserting your viewpoint.

AGGRESSIVE

People who are aggressive communicators are known for expressing their thoughts and feelings often. They tend to dominate conversations at the expense of others. They often speak before they hear another person's full thought, which can negatively affect productivity in the workplace. This communication style may appear to command respect in leadership positions, but it is not a character trait that most people like to be around on a regular basis, which can affect their relationships.

As you develop your communication style, be conscious of not mistaking being aggressive with being a leader. The best leaders can lead without using aggressive tones and tendencies when communicating with others. Great leaders can connect with people through their confident yet personable tone. If you naturally have more of what others have described as an aggressive communication style, it is important to assess your techniques to learn how to balance your tone and physical gestures and research positive communication techniques that may help you overcome some of your aggressive tendencies. If you find yourself lashing out at others and becoming more aggressive, work to reduce stress in your life by incorporating more exercise and social activities or researching things that may make you more confident and reduce anxiety and nervousness in your communication with others, which can sometimes come across as aggression.

PASSIVE-AGGRESSIVE

Passive-aggressive communicators appear passive on the surface, but they often have aggressive motives. While their words sound agreeable, their actions don't align with what they say. They often manipulate situations for their benefit because they feel like they have no other power. This is a very negative communication style, and it is often not tolerated. In the workplace or in video meetings, this can be detected by sarcasm, muttering, fake smiles, or the silent treatment. If you have these tendencies, look for opportunities to openly communicate your thoughts and needs. Find ways to pursue transparent and honest lines of communication to ensure that you feel heard. Take active steps to directly address situations that bother you so that you don't hold things in and then explode later.

ASSERTIVE

Assertive communicators are typically seen as the most productive and respected of all. They share their thoughts and ideas with confidence, but they are respectful and polite. They're happy to take on challenges and additional projects, but they know how to say no when it's necessary. They understand their own limits and protect their boundaries without being overly aggressive or defensive. They make others feel comfortable and are sought out because they can easily facilitate productive conversations. Assertive communicators will typically look directly into your eyes, walk into a room with great posture and confidence, collaborate and share their knowledge with others, and speak with clear messaging.

To improve your assertive communication skills, practice active listening, express your needs and ideas with confidence, encourage others to share their ideas, be open to feedback about your communication strengths and areas for improvement, seek opportunities to practice public speaking, and exercise emotional intelligence. Emotional intelligence is the ability to identify and manage your own emotions and express them in ways that are respectful and helpful to those around you. It also involves understanding the emotions of people around you and responding with supportive and encouraging feedback.

Your professional presence, which includes your style of communication (words and body language), can determine the opportunities you will be invited to participate in, the work you'll be able to do, and the partnerships you will be able to develop. Your communication skills and style are extremely important.

What concerns you the most about your ability to communicate properly?

_____

_____

_____

_____

_____

_____

_____

_____

_____

Considering the four communication styles we reviewed, which would you use to describe yourself?

_____

_____

_____

_____

_____

_____

_____

_____

_____

In what areas of communication can you improve upon your skills (verbal, written, or group presentations)?

_____

_____

_____

_____

_____

_____

_____

_____

Since practice makes perfect, what opportunities do you have at work, home, school, or within your friend group to practice various modes of communication?

_____

_____

_____

_____

_____

_____

_____

_____

_____

_____

Tips: People do not need to know that you are practicing in front of them. Simply use your everyday conversations as opportunities to improve your skills. When you can lead in front of a crowd, do it. At work, when asked to lead a presentation, volunteer. Leaders don't typically lead from behind—so make it a point to find ways to get ahead. You may be interested in becoming an executive who hires others to speak on your behalf so that you don't have to. However, you will still be required to communicate your mission, vision, and goals to them and explain how they will need to complete their tasks.

LEADERSHIP MANAGEMENT STYLES

A leadership management style is a way that someone leads and/or manages a group of people. As we look at some examples, consider the communication style that aligns with each. Even if you're not in an official management position, you may be asked to perform a task or manage a project that will require an effective management style. You must get to know the people on your team so that you understand how to best relate to and communicate with them. There are pros and cons to all, every style will not work with everyone on your team, and the style you use will depend upon the type of work being done. Here are a few, and my suggestion is that you research to find others as you continue to develop:

- Authoritative: Often known for micromanaging (controlling every part of a situation, even small details), this management style tends to dictate exactly what a team is to do every time without question and has high levels of criticism for those who do not comply. Although it creates clearly defined roles and expectations, it can also lead to a decrease in team satisfaction due to the lack of room for professional development and contribution.
- Delegative: This style is often seen as empowering because the manager assigns a task, steps back, and lets their employees do the job according to their knowledge and expertise. Once the task is completed, the manager steps back in to review, give advice, and add improvements. This can foster innovation, but a lack of leadership can cause productivity to suffer.
- Participative: This style creates an environment where managers and staff are all active members of the decision process. They work together to make decisions, and those decisions are highly regarded by the company. This can leave some employees feeling extremely valued and others feeling like they are being asked to do too much.
- Coaching: This management style takes on a true coach approach. The staff is run like a team. The manager is the coach in place to teach, guide, and build their team for the big win. The benefit is that professional development and long-term goals are always at the forefront of the vision for the team. However, there can be so much focus on the team members' and the team's long-term goals that short-term goals suffer.

What management styles are most natural for you? This may help you figure out what type of team or type of work, based on your natural style, that you ultimately want to serve on. It can help you identify which styles you need to develop.

_____

_____

_____

_____

_____

_____

_____

_____

_____

_____

THE EFFECT

It is important to identify the impact your words and conversations will have on those you are talking to in advance. What effect will your conversations have on the next steps for your team, work, and/or partnerships? Remember that your words are weighted. Use them carefully and strategically to build something that is useful to many.

Brand statements are statements that describe your brand:

- I am an aspiring television executive.

- My vision is to develop television content that is reflective of all cultures.
- I will work to create a television network that reflects its audience across the board.

Brand Stamps are impressions that you leave with people, which help them describe you to others, based upon your conversations with them.

You will know you have developed a brand name when someone across the country or in your community speaks highly on your behalf and says, "There is someone who can ..." It is your responsibility to fill in the blank for them during your conversation. For example, after having a conversation about your desire to find a leadership position in a professional organization, someone may talk to a business partner who is looking for someone to serve as a leader in their organization and say, "I met someone amazing the other night who I believe is worth you taking a meeting with." The next thing they share about you should come from what you have strategically shared with them.

Tips

- A lot of the people you meet along the way will be messengers. They will not be *the* person who will hire you or bring you onto a project. They may be able to open doors and introduce you to the right people who will be able to hire you. We'll go further into networking later, but contrary to what people may tell you, it's not all about who you know.
- What's most important is who knows you. When people understand who you are today, what you're building toward, and how you're able to serve as an asset, they will often advertise your brand name to their network, which can lead to new opportunities that will come to find you.
- It's extremely important to have your brand statements drawn out and at the forefront of your mind. Most people only have an attention span of thirty seconds to learn about who you are, like a commercial or a sound bite. You want to make sure that you are giving them a concise, memorable, and relevant message that you

want them to advertise—and that they are excited to share. You never want people to just walk away from you saying you were nice or funny. Leave them with a memorable experience of you that they personally want to reconnect with.

- As a young professional meeting someone who's been in your industry for a long time, you might think you have nothing to offer that would be beneficial to them. However, as someone who has prepared and is able to express yourself as a notable, up-and-coming industry leader, you have a lot to contribute. How you communicate who you are to someone else can motivate them to want to get to know you while you grow so that they are first in line to do business with you once you're ready.

- Make your networking opportunities work for you by learning how to multiply them. If you network successfully with one person—and they are excited about you—they may network with ten more people on your behalf.

STATEMENTS TO BUILD YOUR BRAND

Use the following five statements for questions that you are continuously asked about at networking events, and they will add to your professional scripts. Fill in and edit your answers as you move forward and develop your career road map.

- I'm interested in:

_____

_____

_____

_____

_____

_____

_____

_____

_____

- My career goals are:

_____

_____

_____

_____

_____

_____

_____

_____

_____

- I want to be known for:

_____

_____

_____

_____

_____

_____

_____

_____

_____

_____

- My life's plans and expectations are:

_____

_____

_____

_____

_____

_____

_____

_____

- My life's mission is:

_____

_____

_____

_____

_____

_____

_____

_____

Most of us want to build a legacy or something great within our profession that other people can continue to use after we've retired. However, legacies don't just happen. They are built—brick by brick, project by project, and game by game. Top athletes, lawyers, journalists, and artists have built the legacy and reputation you recognize today. Let's build yours! Ask yourself the following questions and outline specific areas of your vision that will allow you to build a legacy for yourself.

When you retire many years from now, what effect do you want people to say you had on your industry? Think big!

_____

_____

_____

_____

_____

_____

_____

_____

_____

Whether you plan to work at an existing firm or own your own company, how do you want your impact at work to be described by others?

_____

_____

_____

_____

_____

_____

_____

_____

Will your work take you to other communities, countries, or political spaces?

_____

_____

_____

_____

_____

_____

_____

_____

_____

How will the work you do affect your community or the world? I asked someone who made tools for airplanes what impact and/or effect his work had on the world. He initially said, "I mean, I just make the tools." I asked him what would happen if the tools he made malfunctioned during flight. At that point, he realized the effect that his work has on others globally. What local or global effect do your day-to-day actions have?

_____

_____

_____

_____

_____

_____

_____

_____

Tip: Biographies (bios) are used to tell a story about someone:

- Different styles are used for different audiences. Professional bios are used for both executives and nonexecutives. Now, we will be looking at what is typically included for non-executives.

- The intent of a bio is to create a short write-up that quickly explains your most important accomplishments, traits, and qualifications during your career. It's essentially an ad that allows you to tell a short story about who you are, what you've done, and where you're going in a way that is engaging and more compelling to your audience than what they would find in your resume.

- If you don't have a bio, this is a great time to develop one. If your employment history is limited, you can use the highlights from your days in school or affiliations within your community or organizations. Because it's a story, keep your audience in mind. Depending on who you send it to or where you post it, it may need to be tailored so that it tells the parts of your story that the audience you're sending it to is interested in hearing.

- When crafting a professional bio, be intentional about the content you include and modify it according to your objectives. You may wind up using your bio in an email to request an interview for a position that you're interested in. You may also be interested in posting it on your website or social media platforms. On social media, you'll want to be savvy, engaging, and professional. You may, depending on the platform and its requirements, avoid using full sentences to meet the character limits. Some will allow you to include keywords in the form of hashtags that are relevant to your intention for posting it, which will increase the chances that your target audience will discover your profile.

- No matter where you post your bio, keep it professional, do not use abbreviations that are not clear to everyone, and make sure it is consistent with your brand.

My bio says the following about me:

_____

_____

_____

_____

_____

_____

_____

_____

_____

_____

When considering building the reputation of the brand you really want, identify what you are known for now.

What have you made sure people know about you—and how did you do that? Moving forward, it's important to look back and identify what you did in the past to get to where you are so that you can use similar methods to get you where you're going.

_____

_____

_____

_____

_____

_____

_____

_____

_____

How can you upgrade your reputation? Enhancing your reputation requires thoroughly assessing your current reputation so that you can identify what you already have in place. Once you identify where you're going, you'll know which assets you'll need to transfer. Assess what you need to leave behind and what you'll need to add.

I can upgrade my reputation by:

_____

_____

_____

_____

_____

_____

_____

_____

Now that you've taken the time to discover more about who you are and your vision for your future, the next section will get you ready to start setting your expectations for your next level of development. First, identify your key takeaways from this section. Outline your thoughts and plans about your brand development as it stands today and what it is advancing into for tomorrow.

KEY TAKEAWAYS

My key takeaways from this section that I will move into action right now are:

_____

_____

_____

_____

_____

_____

_____

_____

_____

_____

_____

_____

_____

_____

_____

_____

_____

_____

_____

_____

PART II

SETTING YOUR EXPECTATIONS

When preparing for any next step, it is essential to focus on:

- your intent moving forward
- where you need to go
- why you're going there
- what you plan to accomplish while there
- how long you plan to stay

Even for something as simple as going to the grocery store, it is important to prepare before we go so that we do not waste our time or money. Our intent in going to the grocery store is typically to buy food that will help us prepare for the meals we are planning to cook. Making a list and assessing what we need in advance are important.

The same mindset applies to our lives. Making a list of what we need based on where we are going is imperative. It prevents us from filling our time with just anything along the way and prolonging our progress. If you know that you are ultimately going into the store of "professional opportunities" to come out with what you'll need to become a music producer, an engineer, a professional athletic coach, a businessperson, or whatever your goal is, it is necessary that in all your jobs and other professional opportunities, you pick up all the ingredients or skills, experience, contacts, wisdom, and so on that you will need to ultimately make your meal.

We often go into the grocery store hungry and with no plan. Because of that, we come out with things that were placed in front of us on a sales aisle that appear to be the same quality of what we were planning to cook. They seem like they'd be helpful in the long run by saving us time or money. The same applies with our careers. When we have no map of where we'd like to be and how we'd like to serve, and someone offers us a job opportunity that looks good and seems like it will save us time, we'll often buy into it without considering our plans. However, sometimes, just like prepackaged meals that are not as good as the homemade meal we planned to prepare, the quick job offer is not always the same for our growth as sticking to our plan. There are always exceptions to straying from your exact plan. An amazing opportunity might fall into your lap, and it is best to take it. Even in those scenarios, you must make sure it is aligned with your vision or provides some benefit that helps you move ahead.

SELF-ASSESSMENT

When applying for any position, ask yourself two questions:

1. Why am I applying for this opportunity? It's important to ask yourself why you are making a move forward. It does not necessarily mean that you won't make the move after your assessment. It just means that you'll understand the move at a greater level. It often helps you become more successful within the opportunity because you have outlined what success looks like in advance.
2. What do I plan to walk away with? It's necessary to ask yourself what skills, experience, contacts, and knowledge you will gain from this position.

SELF-ASSESSMENT/BRAND STATEMENT DEVELOPMENT EXERCISE

As we continue to work on your brand statements, which will help other people know who you are, what you're looking for, and what you need, I want you to fill in the following:

Tip: Researching and identifying what you need to learn about your next steps will help you add to your professional syllabus. You will be creating a shopping list that will help you look for the knowledge or experience you need to meet your goals.

To be successful within my goals, I need to learn the following:

_____

_____

_____

_____

_____

_____

_____

_____

_____

_____

Tip: Whether you are working at a company now or preparing for a great career, researching companies and positions in your industry is important. Even if you're working in your perfect position, you always want to understand what's happening in your industry. Information about what's trending in other companies can help you bring insights to your team and help you all level up. If you are not in your ideal position yet, identify what's happening at companies within your industry and the positions you're interested in so that you are knowledgeable and are able to have conversations with professionals in your field.

Companies and positions I should research for knowledge and development are:

_____

_____

_____

_____

_____

_____

_____

_____

_____

_____

Tip: When mapping out your career, you can't just consider the job you want. You must also reflect upon your ideal lifestyle and the lifestyle that your ideal job typically provides. If the two don't align, you may find yourself constantly feeling dissatisfied. People don't often talk to young professionals about their plans for their personal lives because they don't want you to become distracted from succeeding in your immediate professional goals. I can understand that. However, it's important to consider the possibilities of what you may want to be included in your future as you start thinking about laying the foundation of your life.

When a high-rise building is being developed, the foundation is set to be able to support all the offices that are in the plan. Even if certain offices never get fully built out, the building itself has the capacity to expand to meet the need of the master plan.

You need to consider all parts of your master plan as you prepare the blueprints for your life because those plans will help you determine what positions (jobs, committees, and volunteer opportunities) you may take.

There are no right or wrong answers for your desires other than what works best for you. However, to reach your goals, you may need to make sacrifices along the way. Rather than being surprised later, you should make yourself aware of what those sacrifices may be before you decide to pour the cement for your foundation.

Some executives have told me they wish they had considered their entire lives before committing to one position. Try to research everything about your ideal life and not just your job since your plans will help you be more balanced personally and professionally. Companies are looking for employees with balanced mindsets who truly want to hold the positions they are being offered rather than employees who are unhappy because their jobs don't balance well with their lives as a whole.

Consider the following:

- Where do you want to live (city, rural, or suburban area)?
- What lifestyle suits you best?
- Do you want a family, children, or a spouse?
- Do you want a job that requires you to travel so that you are guaranteed to see the world? Do you not like to travel at all—or are you only interested in traveling during your personal time?
- Do you like the idea of working in a corner office in a high-rise or working outside in the field and talking to customers?
- Would you rather spend your time on production sets, sports fields as a head coach, or going back and forth on a plane and negotiating deals on behalf of clients?
- It's important to do your research and find out the typical hours required in your ideal position. Will your hours increase or decrease with seniority? In some industries, the senior executives have the benefit of working fewer hours, but in others, their hours increase from forty to eighty hours per week.
- Will you be required to always work in an office—or will you have the flexibility to work from the location of your choice?

You must do your research so that you know what you're signing up for. When starting out, your initial options may be limited—but your goals should not be. These answers will help you make decisions about which jobs to take, people to date, and homes to buy based on your personal goals surrounding the brand that you're building. As you grow and are exposed to new ideas and possibilities, your answers may change, but establishing the baseline of who you are today will help you make solid choices that are aligned with your values and desires.

As a young adult working in the entertainment industry, everyone thought it was odd for me to chime in when they were talking about their families and say I wanted to have a family of my own someday. I did not start planning for my family at that time, but I did make space for the life that I aspired to have. I also made career decisions that allowed me to make room for my life as I saw it in the future. I wanted children and to be able to take them to school and pick them up every day. Thankfully, I was able to develop a brand name, based on my work contributions and habits, which put me in a position of favor to negotiate my wishes into my deal.

Again, companies want employees who are balanced in their personal lives so that they can be excellent professional partners. It is your responsibility to identify what balance will look like in your life. Learn as much as you can about the things you're interested in so that you can make solid decisions now. You can always change your mind and rebrand yourself, but it will take time and sacrifices on your part to do so successfully.

My life's plans and expectations in general are:

_____

_____

_____

_____

_____

_____

_____

_____

_____

EXPOSURE, OPPORTUNITY, AND TRAINING

- Life is an ongoing class that's full of exposure, opportunities, and training.
- You're not going to learn everything in one place, but when you prepare your professional syllabus—no matter where you are—it'll be easier to recognize the development opportunities around you, which will help you graduate to your next level.
- Some of us have been taught that we should be paid immediately in cash for everything we do. Don't let this stop you from volunteering to work on extra projects that could help you grow and gain experience. A lot of the work you do, especially as a young adult, is work that you're doing for yourself—and your payment is growth. That growth, development, and experience will pay you even more in the long run. That growth will hopefully teach you the language of your business and how your industry runs.
- It is important to maintain a proper perspective, focus on your road map, and follow your strategies. What you are exposed to may cause you to change directions or go down unexpected paths, which can be a great thing. Some people find success in multiple areas of business.
- Whatever you decide to do and wherever you decide to go, remember that everything leads you to a destination that is true to some part of who you are. Exposure to new areas of life and business and opportunities to participate at new levels and training and development can elevate your perspective and move you toward success in your career or reveal that what you thought you'd be interested in is not actually for you. Either is a win because they provide insight and put you on track toward your area of excellence.

Focusing on your expectations helps solidify your plans. You'll need your plans in hand as we begin to address how to prepare for future opportunities.

KEY TAKEAWAYS

Focusing on my expectations for my life and lifestyle has helped me realize:

_____

_____

_____

_____

_____

_____

_____

_____

_____

_____

_____

_____

_____

_____

_____

_____

_____

_____

_____

_____

_____

_____

PART III

PREPARING FOR FUTURE OPPORTUNITIES

When preparing for any opportunity, it's important to consider what you are expecting to come out of the opportunity with. In any position, you should be looking to gain new skills and/or heighten the ones you have. You should also prepare for personal growth and enhancing your confidence.

NEW SKILLS

Let's go back to self-assessment. Being aware of who you are and who you are not yet will help you evaluate your needs at every level. You should always be looking to enhance your skill sets. No matter how grand or limited your abilities seem, pay attention to what your skill set needs to be in order to be successful for where you are currently and for where you are going next. You should be looking to enhance your skills at every level of your career. I am going to walk you through seven areas to focus on as they pertain to developing new skills.

Problem-Solving: What is your typical approach to solving problems in team or business settings?

- Problem-solving is an everyday aspect of contributing to the workforce. Companies solve problems for their clients and customers. As a valuable employee or partner, you'll need to have the ability to find the root cause of difficult problems and formulate workable action plans that provide solutions.

- Problem solvers are often creatives who know how to brainstorm and come up with out-of-the-box results. They are known as logical thinkers who are extremely analytical and consider solid methods that are sustainable. They are frequently collaborative, open to hearing the perspective of everyone involved, and sensitive to other people's emotions and viewpoints.

- When solving problems, it is important to identify the exact issue you are looking to solve so that you can stay on track with your results. It is also important to understand the surrounding circumstances. Be sure to research the possibilities for your solutions and poke holes in or test out your ideas to see if they are sustainable. Meet with other people who have dealt with similar challenges and get their opinions if possible. After you have a list of potential solutions, if you are expected to make the final decision on your own, narrow down your options until you find the best fit. If you are working with a team, prepare to present the options and strategize with your team. Once you have made your decision for the approach you are going to take, set strategies for how you intend to execute your plan and implement your solution and then focus on the results.

My typical approach to problem-solving is:

_____

_____

_____

_____

_____

_____

_____

_____

_____

Decision-Making: How confident are you when making decisions? Do you identify the problem, gather relevant information, consider alternatives, weigh the deciding factors, review your decision and the effects, and execute as a part of your standard process?

My decision-making process typically involves:

_____

_____

_____

_____

_____

_____

_____

_____

_____

_____

Judgment: How informed are you when making judgments?

- Are you a critical thinker?
- Do you consider the future and the past when making decisions?
- Do you intentionally take time to listen to others around you, respecting and taking into account their input?
- Do you anticipate the risks associated with your plans?

How would others describe my judgment?

_____

_____

_____

_____

_____

_____

_____

_____

_____

Communication: How can your communication be improved?

- Do you need to increase your knowledge and experience to be a more confident communicator?
- Are you comfortable speaking in front of a crowd?

- Do you look for volunteer opportunities or stretch assignments at work (projects or tasks that are currently beyond your level of knowledge or skill) that put you into a position to practice and improve your skills?

It is important to:

- Prepare ahead of time.
- Listen intensely.
- Be clear and concise in your word choices.
- Utilize emotional intelligence.
- Be aware of your body language, tone of voice, and the perspective that your audience has.

I can improve my communication skills by:

_____

_____

_____

_____

_____

_____

_____

_____

_____

Self-Management: What areas of your self-management do you need to elevate?

Self-management in the workplace is critical because, although we often work in teams, successful teams are formed by individuals who can manage the specific tasks that they contribute to the team.

It is important to:

- understand your professional role and abilities
- align your position with your team effectively
- be strategic in your thinking
- set and stay on track with your priorities
- regulate your emotions
- incorporate self-care regularly

As it pertains to my self-management, I need to elevate:

_____

_____

_____

_____

_____

_____

_____

_____

_____

_____

Collaboration: Effective collaboration requires:

- communicating properly
- reflecting on the long-term effects of an outcome
- crediting others for their contributions
- taking responsibility for mistakes
- being open-minded, organized, and adaptable

Values Clarification: What are some of your values? Do they stem from your family and childhood, your experiences, or religion, culture, travel, or community?

- You need to know how to work with people who do not share your values. Life is not going to place you with people you agree with all of the time, and that's okay. Other people's differences and experiences can teach you about life in ways that you've never imagined. The common ground or task that you are working on collectively can bring you together.
- On the other hand, we all get to determine our own values, and it is extremely important to be clear and outline your personal ethics because they will often lead you to the opportunities that work best for you based on your purpose, mission, vision, goals, and the brand that you're building. They will often sway your decisions and interactions with others consciously or subconsciously. Identifying your values now will help you align yourself with people, opportunities, and causes that are best suited for your drive. In business, many people form relationships and tight bonds based on shared values.

The values that are most important to me are:

_____

_____

_____

_____

_____

_____

_____

_____

_____

_____

Knowledge: Seek knowledge in any opportunity you're presented with. Be strategic and never waste a chance to advance your understanding in an area that you are looking to grow in. Ask yourself, "Why am I here?

What am I supposed to gain from this part of life?" When working with a company or in a partnership, it's important to go in seeking.

Education: What can you learn or understand at a deeper level based on your current or future exposure to your industry of choice?

Having additional exposure can teach me:

_____

_____

_____

_____

_____

_____

_____

_____

Solutions: What solutions have you witnessed in your experience or research about your career have stretched your thinking about your work ahead?

Something I have noticed that is happening in my industry that I found to be interesting is:

_____

_____

_____

_____

_____

_____

_____

_____

_____

Experience: What experiences are you gaining and/or look to gain in your field?

I am excited and looking to gain experiences in my industry that will help me:

_____

_____

_____

_____

_____

_____

_____

_____

Information: What industry information do you have—or will you have—access to by working at a company or organization that will help you grow? Let's talk strategy. This chart highlights eight of the most common positions in most companies. It's important to understand the basics of someone's position so that if you have an opportunity to meet or connect with them in passing, you'll have an idea of at least one area of interest that you can engage with them on.

If someone is the CEO or president, you know that they spend a lot of their time focused on running a business. You have to ask yourself, "If given the opportunity, what can I learn from them? What is on my professional syllabus that they have answers to?" These are points that can be added to conversations, especially when people ask if there is anything they can help you with. Take a good look and keep each position in mind when engaging in conversations. Keep in mind that these are very limited job descriptions, and some positions may vary based on the individual company.

Tip: When networking, don't let your conversations be about you first—unless you are asked. Get to know the other person in general, if possible. The things they share with you can be valuable based on what you're looking to gain insights about. You can ask them how they got into business or what they've learned along the way. Always make your networking process conversational rather than transactional. Everyone understands that what you learn from them may be beneficial, but no one likes to feel like you are using them or standing on their shoulders just to get to your next steps.

CONNECTING WITH GENERAL STAFF MEMBERS	
(CEO) Chief Executive Officer or President	Vice President of Production or Production Manager
(COO) Chief Operating Officer, Vice President of Operations or General Manager	Accountant and/or Bookkeeper
(CFO) Chief Financial Officer & Controller	Office Manager
Vice President of Marketing or Marketing Manager	Receptionist

- CEO (Chief Executive Officer): The highest-ranking executive in a company. A chief executive officer's primary responsibilities include making major corporate decisions, managing the overall operations and resources of the company, acting as the main point of communication between the board directors and corporate operations, and serving as the face of the company.
- President: Primarily responsible for the operational management of a company. In small businesses, the president might be the

owner of the company. In organizations where there is a CEO and a president, the president is second in charge.

- COO (Chief Operating Officer, Vice President of Operations, or General Manager): The chief operating officer (COO) is a senior executive tasked with overseeing the day-to-day administrative and operational functions of a business. The COO typically reports directly to the CEO and is often considered to be second in the chain of command. In some corporations, the COO is known by other terms, including executive vice president of operations, chief operations officer, general manager, or operations director.
- CFO (Chief Financial Officer and Controller): The chief financial officer is responsible for managing the financial actions of a company. The CFO's duties include tracking cash flow and financial planning as well as analyzing the company's financial strengths and weaknesses and proposing corrective actions. The role of a CFO is similar to a treasurer or controller because they are responsible for managing the finance and accounting divisions and for ensuring that the company's financial reports are accurate and completed in a timely manner.
- Vice President of Marketing or Marketing Manager: VPs of marketing take charge of a company's marketing team. They handle strategic brand management, review budgets, set goals, conduct market research, and help maintain an appropriate image of the company.
- Vice President of Production or Production Manager: Plans, directs, and coordinates the development and manufacture of all products made by that company while ensuring that the company uses the most efficient, effective, and economically viable methods for the production of the company's products.
- Accountant: Provides business owners with financial insights based on information gleaned from their bookkeeping data.
- Bookkeeper: Handles the day-to-day tasks of recording financial transactions and data.
- Office Manager or Business Manager: Responsible for overseeing the daily operations of an office and its various departments. Duties include communicating with department heads, relaying

important information or policy changes from upper management, and implementing incentives to enhance employee productivity.

- Receptionist: Duties and responsibilities include greeting visitors, helping them navigate the office, and supplying them with refreshments as they wait. In addition, they sometimes maintain calendars for appointments, sort mail, make copies, and plan travel arrangements.

Tip: The office manager and receptionists are key contacts who are often known as "gatekeepers" or the holders of all knowledge as it pertains to the company. These are often your first points of contact. Get to know them well. When you can't go back to your supervisor for the third time to ask how to use the copier, they should be able to help you.

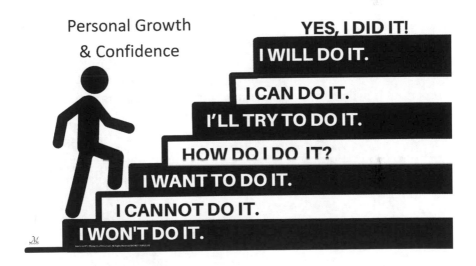

PERSONAL GROWTH AND CONFIDENCE

You should expect to come out of any opportunity with a measure of growth and confidence. Nelson Mandela said, "It always seems impossible until it's done." Oftentimes, when you set big goals, fear can put you in a place of disbelief and convince you that you will not complete what you set out to accomplish. When setting goals, we often go from "I won't" to "I can't," but we still want to do it. Our desire to accomplish our goals in spite of our doubts leads us to asking, "How do I do it?" This is followed by a commitment to try. Once we try, it becomes easier to see that we can do what we set out to accomplish, and that moves us toward getting it done. Next thing we know, we've done it. We have to remember that there are only so many steps from start to finish, and we can achieve our goals one step at a time.

PROPER PERSPECTIVE

Proper perspective brings clarity. One of the issues that young professionals deal with is not understanding certain business norms in their industries. Going into situations with the proper perspective about business norms, protocols, and expectations will allow you to gain more from every situation and be less stressed about what you're being asked to do because you understand the intention behind the request.

As a young professional, remembering that life is a class and your salary is the tuition should help you see your salary as a scholarship. This scholarship is providing an opportunity for your growth in an industry of your choice, and you are continuously learning and developing from the projects, people, and culture around you. Take a moment to identify the areas that you need clarity in as it pertains to your industry. This will be added to your syllabus and interview questions for prospective mentors in the future.

What I need more clarity on as it pertains to business norms in my industry:

_____

_____

_____

_____

_____

_____

_____

_____

_____

Paid Dues

MEMBERSHIP CARDS ENCLOSED

PAYING YOUR DUES

Club memberships are typically very expensive due to the benefits associated with having access to the members and the club. When you are working with a company, it's like having a membership card to a club that you want to be a part of, but you don't fully qualify for the golden package yet. Young adults in entry-level or middle-management positions may say they are just there to "pay their dues." This is not the right attitude to have or project. It makes people feel that you believe you:

- are too good to work with the team you're working with
- don't believe you can learn anything from them
- don't believe they have any networking value

Most of the time, you are paying with your time and effort to work in a position that you either don't qualify for or still need to learn from. Stay humble and confident, remembering that you are there to learn, practice, and serve as you develop.

JOB EXPERIENCE AND JOB OPPORTUNITIES

Whether you are working on a job that is set to be three weeks or three years, you should always be able to walk away with experience, contacts, and future job or partnership opportunities.

Most job interviews, taking multiple interviews into consideration, span from one to five hours. From that, candidates are selected to work in positions that they have no experience in, based solely on the interviewer's interactions with them.

If you are working with people for longer than five hours in a capacity where they have had the opportunity to experience your work ethic, habits, skill sets, and delivery, they should be asking you to stay, come back in the future, or work on a different project with them after you're finished with your current assignment. You have to position your brand to be one that is always in high demand, and if you are leaving, it should only be because it was a temporary position, they are eliminating your position, or you're on to something more aligned with your professional growth. The only way to do that is to do an amazing job at every level. Make sure that your work is stellar—and your personality is too. People work with people who are qualified and likeable. In many industries, people create and work with the same teams on every project because they know they can count on the quality of their work, and their personalities mesh well during long work hours.

GREATER WORK HABITS

To develop greater work habits, assess your current habits, identify your shortcomings and outline—based on your current opportunity—how you can sharpen your skills.

The work habits I need to improve and/or develop are:

_____

_____

_____

_____

_____

_____

_____

_____

STRONGER COMMUNICATIONS SKILLS

Intentionally seek out opportunities to communicate with your coworkers, provide presentations, and be a leader so that you can enhance your abilities in these areas. No one becomes a professional speaker or speaks at an executive level without practice and opportunity. Through your engagement with others, you will learn more about what you need to do to become a stronger communicator, motivator, and leader, and you will also learn more about other people. You will gain knowledge about how to read a room and understand your audience through communication, participation, tone, facial expressions, gestures, body language and posture, eye gaze, and eye contact.

Now that we have outlined areas and ways to prepare for future opportunities, it's time to begin developing your brand. Before we move forward, take a moment to acknowledge the specific ways you need to prepare for your future. What are the next five tasks you will complete in order to move ahead on a more solid foundation?

I will complete the following five tasks to move ahead with a more solid foundation:

1. _____
_____
_____
_____

2. _____
_____
_____
_____

3. _____
_____
_____
_____

4. _____
_____
_____
_____

5. _____
_____
_____
_____

KEY TAKEAWAYS

Focusing on my future opportunities has helped me realize:

_____

_____

_____

_____

_____

_____

_____

_____

_____

_____

_____

_____

_____

_____

_____

_____

_____

_____

_____

_____

_____

_____

_____

_____

PART IV

DEVELOPING YOUR BRAND

It's time to take a deeper dive into developing your professional brand. When developing your brand, always keep your mission, vision, and goals in the forefront of your mind.

BRANDING

IDENTIFY
Long-term **VISIONS**

MAKE
Time for **ASSESSMENTS**

FORM
Action plans that **MOVE**

BRAND
Your **NAME**

BRANDING

Identify your long-term vision: How do you envision carrying out your mission? What will you do, work on, and be involved in?

My long-term vision as it pertains to my career development is:

_____

_____

_____

_____

_____

_____

_____

_____

_____

Make time for self-assessment. Every investment requires a deposit, and every seed needs watering to grow. Your investment and watering will stem from your time and attention. Every successful brand spends time and money on research and development (R&D). In order to grow your brand, you must do the same. Research and development is an important driver of growth since it sparks innovation, invention, and progress.

R&D can lead to breakthroughs for your brand. If nothing else, I suggest that you spend twenty minutes per day or night in quiet time with just you and the masterpiece that you are building to research what you'll need and develop what you have. This is not TV, social media, or friend and family time. It's not the last twenty minutes you spend before your head hits the bed. It is a concentrated period of time to start building your road map. As you begin to get into a great groove in your development, you will begin to desire more than twenty minutes per day. Eventually, it will become an exciting and structured meeting time where you'll invite in strategic partners to join and build with you.

- Form action plans that move. Most people make lists. The problem with a list is that it is typically just a list of thoughts with no room for drawn-out and identifiable actions. Every thought should have supporting goals, and every goal should have tasks attached. Each task should be connected to a timeline of execution dates. Whatever you create should be developed. Whatever is developed should be produced. Whatever is produced should be delivered. What are you creating to be developed, produced, and delivered?
- Brand your name. Everything you know or think about the brands you invest in has been told, shown, or proven to you. Even some of the brands you don't like have shown you why they are not a good fit for you to invest in. You are going to be known by what you do, and you have the ability to affect the narrative by being intentional about what you tell, show, or prove through your day-to-day actions.

My brand name is currently known for:

_____

_____

_____

_____

_____

_____

_____

_____

_____

_____

_____

I am preparing for it to be known for:

_____

_____

_____

_____

_____

_____

_____

_____

Let's start creating your career road map. Take a moment to think through your responses to the following statements while considering any research and development you've done already. Reflect on the work you want to do in your community and in the world. Your answers will affect your vision and your road map.

CREATE A CAREER ROAD MAP

My industry of choice is (if you are still narrowing it down or considering multiple areas of business, write them all down in your notes):

_____

_____

_____

_____

_____

_____

_____

_____

_____

THE EXECUTIVE TRACK

Most industries have an executive track. An executive track is an outline of the positions that are available, from entry-level positions to the most senior positions in that field. A general example is in the area of law. You could become a legal assistant, a secretary, a paralegal, a consultant, an attorney, or a judge. The goal is not to simply obtain the most senior position. The goal is to identify the possibilities and decide which option is tailored best for your mission, vision, goals, and balance in life. Many people think that title and salary are the only determining markers. However, when researching a position, you must consider the big picture and ask yourself the following questions:

- Which position will put me in position to provide what I want to contribute to my industry of choice?
- Which position will allow me to grow into a position that will add the balance I need for my personal life?
- Which position will allow me to be a changemaker if that's what I decide to be?

Research and develop a position that will allow you to contribute to the world in the way you foresee doing so and to accomplish your personal goals.

The executive track (or available options) in my field is:

_____

_____

_____

_____

_____

_____

_____

_____

_____

The position I would like to ultimately serve in is:

_____

_____

_____

_____

_____

_____

_____

_____

_____

_____

_____

What positions do you foresee taking as you move toward your ultimate goal?

My professional goals while working on this track are:

_____

_____

_____

_____

_____

_____

_____

_____

_____

What are you doing, studying, or working on right now?

The current step I'm in is:

_____

_____

_____

_____

_____

_____

_____

_____

_____

_____

My next step is:

_____

_____

_____

_____

_____

_____

_____

_____

_____

PROFESSIONAL FLOWCHARTS

Professional flowcharts help you map out your process. We are going to focus on two types. The first will help you outline specific factors of your brand. We'll look at specific components surrounding who you are personally, professionally, and in conjunction with a company. The second will help you develop your career flowchart, mapping out every area you want to participate in as a professional and as a philanthropist.

Business Components of Your Brand

Personal →	Professional →	In Partnership →
• Appearance • Character & Reputation • Speech & Communication	• Experience • Work Ethics • Organizational Affiliations • Volunteer Services	• Calm under pressure in a stressful environment • Quick in a changing environment

PERSONAL COMPONENTS

With any unknown brand, the first thing we connect with is its label. If you're in a store in another country, don't speak the language, and want to buy a bottle of water, you'll immediately look at the labels. We often make quick decisions based on how a brand looks.

The same thing applies to your professional brand. Your resume, bio, or referral from someone else is often the first "label" that people see wrapped around your brand name. How those things are presented often determines if someone wants to learn more about who you are. When people meet you for an interview, they typically look at several factors that pertain to your "in-person label" or how you carry yourself personally. From your appearance, mannerisms, and communication style, they're often looking to gauge whether or not they believe you'll feel comfortable in the company culture that's already been set.

To be clear, company dress codes and appearance policies are still legal. However, federal law prohibits employers from discriminating against employees based on a number of protected characteristics, including religion, sex, race, and national origin. Company culture is definitely something to think about when considering a position. Generally speaking, different industries have different dress codes based on the work that they do. Someone going to a social media company in a suit and tie to work full-time may not be seen as someone who's going to be comfortable in a laid-back environment. Someone going to a company in jeans and a button-down shirt where suits and ties are the norm—based on the partnerships, meetings, and projects—may have the same issue. When you arrive, company representatives want to know that you understand and will be comfortable in the environment. After you have put together a great label, people will want to learn more about your character and reputation.

After you have connected with the company culture and developed a great reputation based on your character, the next area that will be examined is your communication skills. A leader has the ability to lead others through communication on behalf of their company or to represent the projects they're working on. There are many extremely smart professionals who have more knowledge than anyone else in the room.

However, if they're not willing or able to speak in front of a group and articulate their genius, they could be kept in the background rather than being positioned as a leader.

PROFESSIONAL COMPONENTS

You should be prepared to answer the following questions:

- What experiences do you bring that will benefit the company?
- How will your work ethic serve the team?
- What organizations are you affiliated with that allow you to bring their network into your partnership with the company?
- What volunteer services do you offer on a regular basis? Where and how do you serve?

People often ask about volunteer services to find out if you are someone who gives to a cause that serves others. As you excel in your career and become a salaried employee, it will be expected that you will put in extra time to get the job done without additional accolades or financial compensation.

IN PARTNERSHIP WITH A COMPANY

What areas of your brand will or currently benefit a company, such as communication skills or the ability to relate to people? This exercise will help you develop honest answers that are true to the brand and specific to helping your team. Your answers here can also be used in future job interviews.

Areas of my brand that can be beneficial within a company structure are:

_____

_____

_____

_____

_____

_____

_____

_____

_____

_____

_____

What business components of my brand will work well in partnership with a company? For example, I have the ability to bring calm leadership to stressful environments. When asked about your exceptional differences, never provide standard practices like stating that you're loyal, punctual, or a team player, as those are to be expected.

Components of my brand that will work well in partnership with a company are:

_____

_____

_____

_____

_____

_____

_____

_____

_____

_____

DEVELOPING YOUR CAREER FLOWCHART

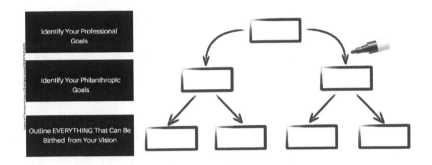

YOUR CAREER FLOWCHART

You'll be able to incorporate what you draft from this exercise into your professional development process immediately. Your flowchart is a tool that serves as a blueprint. It outlines everything you envision being incorporated into the lifetime and legacy of your professional career. It can be easy to forget that you're building a brand with a purpose, but this will serve as a visual reminder and focal point that you can print out and hang up in your work area. What you develop today is something that you will utilize and expand on for years to come.

My company is still producing projects that were added to our flowchart when it was created more than ten years ago. Taking the time to focus on building a blueprint for how our company would flow, adding everything I could envision, and making room for it encouraged me to develop content and programming in those areas. I built our content based on the vision for the brand before the customers and clients came forward. I took the time to prepare for what I believed would happen. Our flowchart eventually became our company deck, which is a PowerPoint presentation that outlines the details of every project listed on the flowchart. It has given us a clear direction to follow. Each page is like a card in a deck of cards. You will not share your full deck with everyone you meet. You will share specific pages of the PowerPoint presentation that outline projects that align with the potential partners you meet with as you determine if they will be the right partner to work with you on that project. When business offers started coming in, the flowchart made it easier to confirm whether those deals were truly aligned with our vision and what we had set out to accomplish. Nothing happens overnight. Some of the projects on our flowchart are still in the queue to be produced, some are in development, and some are in the market. They are all, however, based on the mission of our brand.

On your chart, you'll outline your professional and philanthropic or charitable plans as well as any interests that can branch out from those goals. This will help you reiterate your intentions, vision, and strategies. It will give you a clear visual of the categories within your professional plans and serve as a guide to help you identify the research, development, and networking you'll need to invest in each category. If you can look at your flowchart as a career road map and foresee where you're going, you can identify a list of what you're going to need as you move along on your trip. When you create this list of the people, experiences, and knowledge you'll need on your journey, you'll start looking for what you've identified as you move forward.

It's as if I told you that you are about to play a game where the board represents your entire life, and the objective is to make it around the board or through your life having picked up everything that was associated with who you are.

There are two challenges in this game:

1. Recognizing the many aspects of your identity before you really start playing in the game of life so that you know what you're looking for
2. Having the fewest number of setbacks as possible (if you don't know who you are, you won't know what to pick up along the way)

Building your flowchart is not about accomplishing everything right now. It is about having a great understanding of what will be accomplished later, based on what you can see today. Once you've finished your chart, you should be able to share this information in a sixty-second presentation with anyone who is interested in learning about your professional aspirations.

It will also help you:

- design your complete career blueprint as you imagine it today
- identify what you can focus on and accomplish right now
- understand how you can expand it in the future

Let's look at a few examples, keeping in mind that everyone's chart will be different because although career interests may be similar, the details of how each person wants to participate in their industry may be different. If you're interested in becoming a marketing executive and have an interest in writing and speaking, you may decide to become an expert in marketing and eventually write a book or contribute to a business journal to share what you've learned. You may decide to be a local or international speaker. When assisting my clients with building their flowcharts, I always ask, "What's your give?" Giving when you receive keeps you balanced and helps you grow. What is your giveback? What are you learning to give away to others? Where do you want to give? Are you interested in building, funding, or contributing to a nonprofit? Will it be one that aligns with your professional industry, your community, or both? Whatever it is, you get to decide how you want to add to the benefit of others.

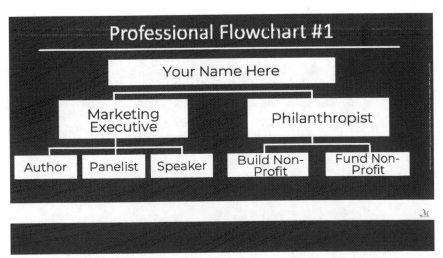

As an artist, you may decide that you want to perform and be an entrepreneur who owns your own studio where you support other artists as they build up their talents. On the nonprofit side, you may decide to donate time to teach or perform for others.

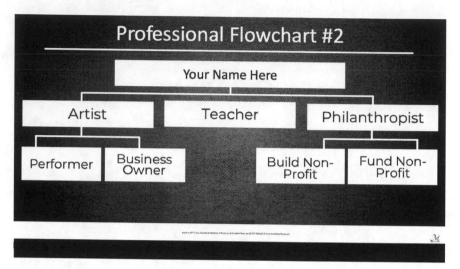

As a civil engineer, you may decide to be an international expert, a city representative, or even a business owner. Based on your interests in business, you may own a consulting engineering firm that manages other engineering projects. On the nonprofit side, you may want to work with children and introduce them to the possibilities and importance of engineering.

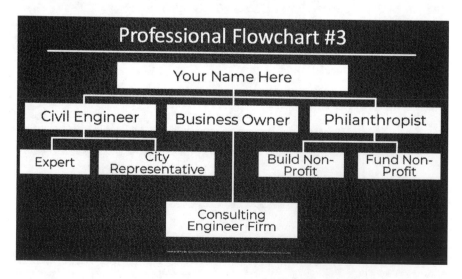

Tip: It's important to recognize that everybody will not see or understand the details of your vision. Not everyone has the same prescription for life to see things through the same lens that you do. It doesn't necessarily mean that they don't support you. It just means that you need to align yourself with people who have the ability to see the possibilities of what you see. Your plans for what you are going to provide for the world are a gift that you can't share with everyone during your planning stages. Not everyone will be able to process your ability to succeed, and because we communicate to make actions happen—receiving emotional support or guidance—it's important to be intentional with who, what, and why you share as you move forward.

Many people will project their inabilities on to you, think that you're scatterbrained, or tell you that you are doing too much. It's your job to keep pushing toward what you believe you can do. If you're planning, build big and find other builders who are happy to walk you through the process of what you should expect and prepare for. Find mentors who are happy to share their knowledge but understand that there are expectations and often requirements for mentorship. I tell my mentees all the time that my standards for mentorship are that I am going to coach and advise you based on what you tell me you want to do. Then you'll come back when you have questions or have done the assignments that I give and are ready for the next step. Professionals who mentor you should never have to run after you to give you a gift or transfer knowledge to you. Be ready to take their advice, run with it, and come back to them when you've completed your task and are ready for your next step.

If you decide that you only want to pursue one area of one profession, that is OK. If you decide that you want to build an enterprise based on all of your talents, that's OK too. You just have to be organized, diligent, focused, and patient with yourself, remembering that buildings are sometimes built brick by brick. The bricks at the bottom are often more important than those at the top because they serve as the foundation. Don't rush through your process. After you answer the questions below, you will be able to give a presentation like the following but based on the specific goals you've drafted:

Hi, my name is_____. I am a current (or an aspiring) civil engineer. My goal is to become an expert in my field where I can serve as a city representative. At some point in my career, I plan to open a consulting engineering firm where we will hire engineers to partner their skills with the projects that we take on. On the philanthropic side, I am interested in finding programs and organizations where I can donate my time to young engineers who are looking to gain insights about the industry.

My professional vision is to:

_____

_____

_____

_____

_____

_____

_____

_____

My immediate goals are to:

_____

_____

_____

_____

_____

_____

_____

_____

_____

The following is what can be expanded from my goals:

_____

_____

_____

_____

_____

_____

_____

_____

_____

My philanthropic ambition is:

_____

_____

_____

_____

_____

_____

_____

_____

_____

_____

Your professional flowchart is going to tremendously enhance your ability to network. If you understand who you are and where you're going, you won't have to concentrate on remembering what you are going to say when you meet people. You can be more in tune with learning about your new contact and focusing on any questions they may throw your way. After you have developed your brand to a level that you are comfortable promoting, you can begin to incorporate it into your new networking plan.

KEY TAKEAWAYS

This section on brand development has helped me:

_____

_____

_____

_____

_____

_____

_____

_____

_____

_____

_____

_____

_____

_____

_____

_____

_____

_____

_____

_____

_____

_____

_____

_____

PART V

NETWORKING EFFECTIVELY

Networking is the exchange of information, ideas, or services among individuals, groups, or institutions with common professional or special interests. For the sake of our work together, let's focus specifically on networking as it pertains to the cultivation of productive relationships for employment or business.

- Networks are created to be mutually beneficial and built over time by developing relationships that allow you to:
  - understand other people's interests and needs
  - share your interests and needs

- As you continue to meet new people, be sure to ask the right questions to determine if someone might serve as:
  - a great strategic partner in your immediate network who you will connect with often based on how you support each other
  - someone you have access to in the event you need them but do not need to connect with them frequently

- Networking is not about collecting friendships or followers, although you may over time get those added benefits. It is, however, about coming together to accomplish like-minded missions.

As it pertains to networking, the greatest challenge for young and seasoned professionals is the ability to know themselves enough to appropriately introduce who they are to others based on their backgrounds and what they really want to do next. In other words, many are not certain of:

- who they really are beyond who they've been
- what they want their next step to be
- how they want to be perceived in their network
- what they need to do to accomplish their goals
- what legacy they intend to leave
- how they should articulate their message based on how it may serve the person they are speaking with

When you think about attending a company- or industry-related event where there may be hundreds of people to meet, what is your greatest challenge when considering networking for your next level?

My greatest challenge when considering networking for my next level is:

_____

_____

_____

_____

_____

_____

_____

_____

_____

Tips: When intentionally setting up your network, strategy is key. Every part of your story is not going to be interesting or useful to everyone. Networking is often like going fishing. Before you arrive on the boat or show up at a networking event, you should always study the waters. Know the kinds of fish (or people) who will be there *and* what kind of food (or types of people and/or opportunities) they may be looking for so that you can prepare to serve them and bring them on board with you.

Although you may meet random people who can connect you to opportunities along the way, when growing in business, it's important to be intentional with your networking efforts. You will probably spend a lot of your time getting to know others at professional events. Depending on your industry and where your industry leaders spend time connecting, you may find yourself buying tickets for galas, dinners, concerts, or sporting events. Networking events can be an expensive investment. When you're prepared and understand which investments work best for you, they can pay off with a great return on your investment (ROI). Let's say you get invited to three incredible events that are scheduled for the same evening. Even if you're gifted with complimentary tickets, you will have to decide which event is more beneficially aligned with your long-term plans. What's your best projected ROI?

Industry events are often fun, but you have to decide if spending your time there will cost you time away from a more relevant business event where you could be building relationships and business opportunities, time with family, or much-needed rest to prepare for a project. Many executives have a yearly budget that allows them to go to business events to build and market their companies. If each event costs five hundred dollars per seat, and they have a budget of two thousand dollars, they will be limited to four events per year out of perhaps one hundred that may be available. In business, we must make calculated decisions about where and how we maximize our time.

Before attending an event, prepare a brief overview of your introduction that captures your mission and reason for attending.

- Research to gain as much knowledge on who will be present:
  - People are typically listening for commonalities in your introduction that will allow them to connect with you in the future. Your answers should be true to brand and tailored,

when possible, around the type of event you are attending and who you're speaking with.

- Even if it's a family BBQ that may include outside influencers, know who will be there so that you can prepare to connect with people at a higher level.

- Get to know your family members as an adult. Ask questions about their careers and life paths. You'd be surprised to learn that your aunt who you only know as your aunt, based on her professional experience, is actually able to help you grow into the next level of your career. Heighten your conversations so that people you already know begin to understand that they can engage with you on a new level. This may make them feel comfortable about referring or hiring you. Don't miss an opportunity to serve the people who are closest to you.

- Encourage people to speak first about their life and listen more than you talk. Even if you're asked to start a conversation, you can:
  - Provided that it's not an event designed for super speedy introductions, begin with a brief intro. You could say, "Hi my name is _____. I am an aspiring _____." Depending on the event, instead of "I am an aspiring ..." you could say anything that aligns with the organization, such as, "I've been a member here since ..."
  - Then, you can turn it over to them by saying, "I would love to learn more about your work." People who are able to listen to others and quickly find ways to support them are valuable in all industries because they are able to process information quickly and strategize potential plans based on their resources. If you listen to others, you'll know if a part of who you are might connect with the person you're talking to in a way that serves a need and excites them to learn more about you.

Most people have not taken the time to assess who they are beyond their current title and degree. It's completely understandable that when people spend ten years working hard to obtain a certain position—along with balancing family, friends, and a social life—they might not have tried to strategically build out their brand. I want you to do this work now so that you can develop an exceptional mindset among your colleagues. When networking, keep the destination that you have on your career road map in mind, but be open about how you might get there.

Tip: Moving forward on your path can be like traveling. You may plan to take a train but meet someone at an event who has plane tickets that can get you there quicker—or you could plan to take a flight that gets canceled, which leads you to a bus, sitting next to someone who could move your journey onto on a brand-new route.

- Know yourself thoroughly.
- Know what you know.
- Know what you don't know.
- Know what you are open to.
- Know what you're not open to.

When opportunities arise, it will be easier to make the best decisions that will work for you.

When networking, develop a keen ear to recognize any options that may be right in front of you in case you have an opportunity to make a shift in how you travel to your destination. Always work toward an exceptional plan A while being aware of an awesome plan B and preparing your skill sets for a plan C that may come by way of an option that you didn't even know exists. Along the way, on your journey to your destination of building a legacy, the roads—or ways that you plan to get there—may change based on your experience, exposure, and opportunities. Your job is to make sure you arrive in a place that is connected to who you are.

NET VERSUS GROSS

At networking events, think about *net versus gross* and how it relates to your paycheck. When your employer offers you one thousand dollars a week, that is your *gross amount*. However, what you take home after taxes and other deductions is your *net pay*. This is the amount that you've worked hard for and get to put in your net to utilize for your benefit. When walking into a networking event, don't feel as though you need to take everyone's contact information home with you. Research before you get there and try to connect with those you are planning to put in your net and build a relationship with.

If you're looking to connect with an executive at a specific company but are unable to, try to connect with someone on their team in hopes of learning how you may eventually connect with them. If you are unable to find out who is going to be in the room, try to have short but engaging conversations with as many people as possible without coming across as being in a rush. The key is to build meaningful experiences through brief conversations that will be intriguing enough to make people want to continue speaking with you at a later date.

KEY TOOLS: SELF-ASSESSMENT, SOUND BITES, AND SOCIAL MEDIA NETWORKING SITES

Developing and producing your professional scripts will enable you to have available content that you can highlight, edit, and share with others as sound bites. When speaking about your plans in a general sense, if you intend to serve in multiple positions across the life of your career, be prepared to express how each position connects with your personal mission and overall vision. This will prevent you from coming across as being scatterbrained.

You don't need to share all of your life's plans with everyone. Instead, share information about your plans as you deem necessary, based on who they are and how they may connect with parts of your plans. Make sure that your social media networking sites are reflective of your brand and professional scripts. These days, everything is instant, and few people carry business cards. People will literally ask you in the middle of your conversation if you are on the top business social media networking site and will check if your conversation is consistent with what you have listed on the business site while you are standing there. Make sure you develop your online presence before you start networking on a large scale because you will be tested.

NETWORKING TIPS

- Every conversation is an interview.

- Understand the psychology behind the questions and your intent behind your answers.

- It's not all about who you know, but who knows you.

- Become an important referral.

Every conversation is an interview. When someone is engaged in a conversation with you, they are taking mental notes for one reason or another and applying them to the thought of possibly interacting with you again. Be true to your answers so that regardless of the outcome of your interaction, you leave them with a good sense of your thoughts.

LEARN THE LANGUAGE OF YOUR BUSINESS: FLUENCY, FACTS, AND TRENDS

Fluency: No matter what industry you work in, it is important to learn the specific language of your business and be fluent in it. Be familiar with the terminology and learn how to use it appropriately. As with any language, in business, people will recognize your level of knowledge based on whether you speak with ease and understand specific terms. Just like when speaking Spanish to someone who is fluent, they can tell if you have taken Spanish 1 or Spanish 4—or if it seems to be something that is natural to you.

The same thing applies in business. People in your industry are able to determine your level of expertise based on how you respond to their questions. For instance, if you are in TV production, and someone says that the show is going on hiatus, you should know that means the production will be shutting down for a break.

TRUTH AND TRUST

I've met many people who have misrepresented their professional positioning by intentionally answering questions with very general responses in hopes of seeming more experienced than they are. However, anyone who is familiar with their industry would be able to identify if what they're saying is true by asking some basic questions. Truth and trust are essential in building relationships and stretching the truth or getting caught in a lie can destroy any possibility of developing rapport with someone. When people in Los Angeles introduce themselves as TV producers, I ask, "What type of producer are you: an executive producer, a line producer, or a consulting producer?" It is easy to determine if someone is sincere if they understand the industry terminology. Always answer honestly and with integrity and never assume that just because you're talking to a doctor, they are not familiar or affiliated with other professions.

INSIGHT

Being fluent in terminology and being knowledgeable about the roles within certain professions will help you navigate your conversations. If you meet someone who says they are an engineer, asking them what type of engineer they are may allow you to quickly develop a strong connection. You can ask questions that are specific to their expertise, the types of projects they are working on, and what they plan to do next.

FACTS AND TRENDS

Stay alert about trends in your industry. Know the difference between facts, opinions, and gossip so that you can contribute to conversations on multiple levels. Be an asset because of your awareness of industry trends and updates. Be knowledgeable—but don't be a know-it-all. This requires the skill of knowing how to read a room or have the emotional intelligence to understand when your insight is needed, wanted, and valuable.

Know when to end a conversation and reserve the rest of your thoughts for your next meeting. It's important to know when you've said enough during your first conversation. When you're at a large event and have a limited time to network, your goal is to make enough of a genuine connection with your contacts to get them to invite you to set a meeting to discuss things further. Don't oversell yourself. Once your contact has expressed an interest, get their contact information and prepare to move on. You have to know how to have a sense of when to leave a conversation when it's still on a high note. Many great salespeople have had to learn the hard lesson of not talking themselves out of a sale and/or deal.

- Know the psychology behind their questions and the intent behind your answers. Always ask yourself, "Why is this person asking me this question as it pertains to the possibility of us working together or staying connected? How will my answer affect the outcome of our conversation?"

- It's less about who you know and more about who knows you. People often say it's all about who you know. What's more important is who knows you. There is no question that it is wonderful to have people in your life who you can call on when you need a resource. However, it's a greater asset to have people who know and believe in what you stand for so much so that they will call you to bring you resources without you having to ask. That only happens when you have built a well-defined brand name that people want to be connected to. They may not be someone in your industry, but because they support your mission, anytime someone in their network who is in your industry brings up anything related to what you are doing or plan to do, they will mention you. Make sure that everyone around you understands why they should know you—and stay consistent in your positioning.

- Become an important referral. Everybody wants to know about a good thing or a great person. Bragging about who people are connected to seems to be human nature. When people leave your presence, they should want to introduce or refer you to someone else based on your time spent with them. It doesn't matter if your conversation with them is five minutes or fifty minutes. Your presence, confidence, humility, ability to connect, and knowledge should be intriguing.

When networking, what are you looking for?

NETWORKING
- Industry Knowledge
- Strategic Partners
- Deals, Expansions, & Professional Opportunities
- Transferring of Knowledge
- Building Brand Awareness

When you're networking, look for these six areas of interest:

INDUSTRY KNOWLEDGE

Industry knowledge is a collection of knowledge and an awareness of the details about what is happening within specific industries. Knowing about various developments, current trends, and challenges in your industry allows you to deliver more impressive projects and presentations for your company. Staying updated about changes in your industry can help you improve your career. When networking with industry leaders, listen for and ask questions about knowledge that pertains to your specific industry, company, or position. Although having information about general career development is an asset, there is a bonus to gaining insights about industry knowledge.

Recognizing how your company has evolved can add to your strategy as you prepare to provide solutions. If you are being asked to solve a problem for your team and are aware of what has been tried in the past—what has and has not worked in your company and your industry—that information will help you structure what you offer as a solution. Outside of networking events, be sure to connect with and/or join *employee resource groups* (ERGs) at your company because members are often well informed about industry trends and historical changes. Follow industry leaders on social media, subscribe to trade magazines, blogs, and newsletters, and watch webinars and listen to podcasts to learn more. Don't forget to ask your human resources representative who they believe you might learn from at your company so that you can arrange for occasional informational meetings with those colleagues to learn more.

STRATEGIC PARTNERS

A strategic partnership is typically formed when a company or organization makes an arrangement to work with or help another so that it is easier for each of them to achieve their goals.

The same idea works for individuals. No one succeeds at an extremely high level alone. Deliberately seek out partners who can add insight to your process and/or the production of whatever you are looking to produce. Prepare to add insight to their process as well in hopes that your partnership will be beneficial to you both—as well as to your industry or companies. Look for people who have similar positions, goals, and interests as you build your network so that you can work on some projects together. At the least this will give you access to people who speak the same language as you, which will allow you to have someone to work with, practice with, and increase your business language skills.

Tip: Be sure that there are no conflicts of interest in your strategic partnerships. A conflict of interest occurs when an individual's personal or business interests could compromise another's. Networking with someone outside of your company who is building the same type of product you're building and sharing industry secrets could affect the outcome of your business. It is great to be connected to people who are in the same business, but it's imperative to use discretion in what you share.

Seek people in executive positions who have been where you are going so that you can learn from them through their past and present experiences. Ask them how you might serve as an asset to them. They might want you to provide insight to them as a young professional who has some industry knowledge and a fresh perspective. Always consider how you can have a positive impact on and provide some form of service for those who have a positive influence on you.

DEALS, EXPANSIONS, AND PROFESSIONAL OPPORTUNITIES

When networking, listen to learn about the needs of others. Their needs could turn into potential business deals, partnerships, expansions, or professional opportunities for you and/or your company.

TRANSFERRING OF KNOWLEDGE

Knowledge transfer is the process of conveying important information from one part of a company or person to another, and when it is done correctly, it increases the efficiency and productivity of an organization. When employees have worked in the same positions for a long time because they are so good at their jobs, no one else at the company might know how their jobs are actually done. If they quit or become sick, no one else will know their processes. There might not be a job description or a training manual because they just went through their daily tasks with no script.

When asked to participate in a knowledge-transfer project, always take the opportunity. You may think, *That's not my job. I don't need to have all that information.* When you are being paid to learn, take the extra classes when you can because you never know how industry information will add to your journey. If you are on the receiving side of a knowledge-transfer project, you may be gifted with a large download of information in a very short period of time that would have taken you years to obtain otherwise. If you are transferring information, remember that part of your goal is to enhance your organization's performance by helping to organize, create, capture, or distribute knowledge and ensure its availability for future users.

BUILDING BRAND AWARENESS

You may have an amazing personality that everyone likes and wants to brag about. However, you have to decide whether you want people to advertise your personality alone or your leadership vision and plans. Networking allows you to provide quick sound bites or commercials that help you multiply an awareness of your brand to others. Take time to develop your messaging because people might take your message and run with it and tell everyone they know you. However, they might love your personality, but if you didn't give them anything to take with them to advertise to others, they might suggest someone else as a better referral for their network.

LOCAL, NATIONAL, AND INTERNATIONAL NETWORKING OPPORTUNITIES

It's imperative to find ways to network locally because networking in your city will typically allow you to have more frequent hands-on growth and leadership experiences. Make an effort to ask around about opportunities that will take you beyond your current scope of influence. Think about national and international possibilities. With virtual opportunities becoming more common, there are no limits to where you can network. Networking with other professionals will elevate your business game by providing real-life, hands-on experiences to learn from. You can contribute to panel discussions, group sessions, and more, which you can add to your resume and professional bio.

Marketing is a significant part of professional brand development. It is the action of promoting who you are and what you have to offer to others through your services, content, and/or products.

Market research requires thoroughly gathering data about the market (people, companies, and/or industries) that you're taking a deeper dive into. Analyze the market to better understand what that group of people needs so you will know how you can best serve them.

Use advertising to communicate to your audience and promote your brand in order to attract interest, engagement, and opportunities. It can require a major investment of time, effort, and money. It is not something you want to approach without a set plan because rebranding requires a greater effort, and it is not always effective. There are certain people who will not give you an opportunity to "re-present" yourself to them. Don't rush the process—but don't delay it either. Start developing today.

Developing a plan, even if you don't use every part of it, will help you tremendously through the process. People often think that they can always figure things out as they go along. There's a popular saying in business for when there has been a lack of time to develop a plan: "We're building the plane while we are flying it." This can be necessary at times, depending on the opportunity that has been presented. It works sometimes, but it is absolutely not ideal. If we are building the plane while we are flying it, our flight is probably not going to be as smooth as it could have been if we had taken the time to fully prepare for takeoff.

When building a marketing plan, start by identifying your brand's mission and/or the drive behind the marketing plan. Why do you want to drive people to you? What will they receive? What will they give? Marketing is about strategy. Marketing strategy is a process that can allow a brand to concentrate its limited resources on the greatest prospects to increase opportunities and achieve a sustainable competitive advantage.

Take a little time to think about your strategic marketing plan. Let's look at six basic areas to consider.

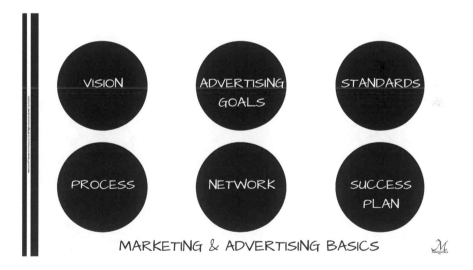

MARKETING & ADVERTISING BASICS

VISION

When deciding on a plan for your traditional and social media networking and marketing, make time for a strategy session first and outline your vision for your best conceivable outcome and return on your investment. When you think about marketing and advertising your brand to your current and/or potential network, what is the vision for your best case-scenario?

My vision is that I will create a marketing plan that delivers these results and includes:

_____

_____

_____

_____

_____

_____

_____

_____

_____

PROCESS

A marketing plan is not just posting on social media every day or planning to attend ten industry events. It has more to do with the big picture and the small details of the who, what, when, where, and why of your process. Think of everything you do as building blocks.

Who should your current target audience be, considering your long-term goals? As you grow and evolve, so will your audience. What kind of people should you speak to and present yourself to now in order to establish yourself in the market for the long run?

- Industry leaders who will want you to serve as an asset to their teams?
- Young professionals who are your peers, colleagues, and the next generation of leaders?

- Organizational leaders who may ask you to sit on a panel and/or committee to discuss your thoughts about your industry?

It's great to have a lot of general supporters. However, when you're building a marketing strategy, because you have to spend so much time, effort, and sometimes money in acquiring each follower or subscriber, you want to make sure that you are getting a good return on your investment. Work to acquire people who align with your brand's mission so that you can eventually turn your followers into business partnerships, clients, or customers. Having followers or subscribers who don't add to your ROI because perhaps they don't understand the benefits of what you're providing or have no intention of contributing to what you're doing is like having one hundred people outside a theater who show up but don't buy tickets. You want to make sure that you have the right audience for your offer.

My audience should be:

_____

_____

_____

_____

_____

_____

_____

_____

_____

In five years, leaders in your industry should be able to look back at your online presence and find a consistent history of your contributions. Based on your plans, what will they say when considering why you should be selected for the next promotion or committee?

Tip: When you are asking or negotiating for a promotion or new leadership position, you have to identify how your promotion will advance your career and benefit your company or industry. For instance, someone might say, "Promoting me into to a managerial position will allow me to do, create, implement, execute, and serve at a higher more productive level." Make sure you consider the big picture of why your elevation will benefit everyone involved.

Based on my plans, in five years, industry leaders will be able to look back at my online presence and say I am a great candidate for a leadership role based on:

_____

_____

_____

_____

_____

_____

_____

_____

_____

What are you—or will you be—marketing yourself as online and at events?

_____

_____

_____

_____

_____

_____

_____

_____

_____

_____

Tip: As a professional, there will be times when you will look to "receive" or be nominated for leadership positions. You can take the lead now by adding your voice and contributing to conversations online that pertain to your industry, its trends and changes, adding an educated, fresh perspective. Most things that you contribute to, especially online, will be added to the internet and will help you build your online portfolio. Generally, whenever someone searches your name online, everything you've contributed to will pop up, which adds to the credibility of your brand. At the same time, be very intentional about what you lend your voice to because once your quote is on the internet, it is almost impossible to get it removed. What does or will your voice add to your industry and community?

- What do you intend to talk about?
- What is your brand voice or the unique way that you present your thoughts to the world?
- What is your tone?
- What viewpoints should people expect from you?

Tip: You don't have to provide the same points of view all of the time, but there should be something (expertise or insights) consistent that your audience comes to you for and expects from you. You don't want to be known for being inconsistent and all over the place. You have to determine an approach that will be most beneficial for you.

My audience, industry, and community should expect the following from me:

_____

_____

_____

_____

_____

_____

_____

_____

_____

When will you get started with your strategic plan? Based on your schedule, when and how often do you intend to update your strategy, post content, and attend events to add to your growth plan?

Tip: Unless you are a professional blogger or someone who gets paid to post every day, do not feel an unnecessary need to post. Marketing is advertising what you are doing and/or have built. The main point is to do your work to build. Set clear boundaries for yourself as it pertains to the time you allot for marketing your brand. The CEO of a million-dollar company is typically *not* posting every day! They post when they have something to advertise based on the work they have already done.

The date I intent to start preparing my strategic plan is _____. Based on my schedule, I will contribute to my growth plan on a(n) _____ basis."

Where do you plan to contribute your voice? Which events, organizations, blogs, conferences, or teams at work will you add to your plan as a strategic partner to fulfill your mission?

Tip: Once you do your research and identify where you want to contribute your thoughts, be sure to have your bio and brand statements ready to share. Create a tailored bio that's 250 words or less, is true to your brand, and aligns with their mission. With your strategy in hand and research done on the partner you'd like to work with, it should be easy to send each potential partner an email with your bio, stating that you love the work that they are doing, would like to learn more, and want to discuss how you might serve as an asset to their work.

I plan to add the following organizations, blogs, and conferences to my strategic plan:

_____

_____

_____

_____

_____

_____

_____

_____

_____

How much money do you intend to invest in your marketing plan for events and subscriptions?

Tip: Research what events are happening and what marketing tools may help to enhance your process. With so many free apps, there's a chance that if you're really resourceful, you will not need to spend any money. If you cannot afford to buy tickets to a networking dinner, many organizations will allow you to attend for free if you volunteer to assist. You do not have to sit at a table and eat a meal like everyone else to learn. You just have to find a way to be in the room.

Since many organizations select their volunteers months in advance, reach out as soon as you find out about the event if you are interested in volunteering. Always find out if an event you want to attend has scholarships or a discounted ticket price if you need assistance. The goal is to be in the room to listen and learn. Some events offer free live streaming. Do your research to find out what is available.

I may need to invest the following amount of money based on my research:

_____

_____

_____

_____

_____

_____

_____

_____

_____

Every strategic plan has to have checks and balances. Get into the habit of always asking yourself, "Why?"

- Why am I doing this particular task or project? Sometimes we do something because it is the standard in our industry, but that doesn't mean it works best for our brand. Innovation, although it's not always necessary, creates new standards. Strategy always prompts the question why.
- Why am I going to this particular event?
- Why am I posting on this particular blog?
- Why am I investing in this particular social media marketing? Always ask yourself why and outline the effect.

Advertising goals are the targets that brands set to achieve through their marketing efforts. As you build your brand, make sure that your efforts:

- increase your brand awareness
- generate high-quality leads, contacts and partnerships
- establish you in your industry as an up-and-coming young professional

- increase and align your social media presence with the mission of your marketing campaign
- boost brand engagement (the process of building and sustaining a commitment from your contacts, clients, and/or customers to your brand)
- increase your professional positioning

Boosting brand awareness has to do with engaging with your network in a way that makes them want to stay involved with you and/or share your name with their network as a referral.

Everything that you build in your marketing plan should increase your ability to take your next solid step forward. Do what you need to do to get where you need to get with drive and integrity. Your mission and/or the purpose of why you're doing your work will drive you forward, your faith will keep you going, and your integrity will help secure your spot.

NETWORKING

The people and organizations at the top of my list to connect with are:

_____

_____

_____

_____

_____

_____

_____

_____

_____

_____

_____

STANDARDS

Some marketing campaigns set very high standards and stay consistent with their vision, and some do not. What will your marketing standards be? Presentation is crucial.

- Does your current traditional and social media marketing represent who you were, who you are, or who you will be? Is it a perfect blend of all three?
- Does the label you wear—not the clothes you wear but how you present yourself in person or online—truly represent your brand?
- Does your online color scheme represent your industry and energy? You have to think about the little things when you design your plans because they help you connect with your audience and/or network.
- Proper grammar is considered elementary. Having control of your spelling and sentence structure in conversations, emails, business text messages, and your online presence shows your attention to details.

You have access to research and can review marketing examples. You do not have to duplicate what somebody else is doing, but you can learn what has been successful in the market before and see what can work for your core audience by incorporating what's necessary for your market and tailoring it to your brand.

PLANNING FOR SUCCESS

Marketing metrics are significant because they help brands determine whether their campaigns are successful, and they provide insights that help them adjust their future campaigns accordingly.

Plans for success always begin with an end goal in mind. Start with a clear goal and objective. Decide what metrics or key performance indicators (KPIs are a quantifiable measure of performance over a time for a specific objective) you'll need in place to monitor your marketing campaign's effectiveness. Establish a time frame and schedule to monitor results. Collect data from all of your sources and feedback from all those who are experiencing your marketing campaign. Examples of metrics for social media are follower count, impressions or reach, and engagement rate.

When considering content marketing, we look at blog traffic, amount of content shared, and content downloads. For videos, we consider impressions and total viewing time.

Tips

- Make it effortless for your audience to connect with your brand.
- Use social media platforms that work best for your brand.
- Develop a compelling brand story that is unique and captivating.
- Create a clear call to action so that your audience knows what they are there to do or how they should participate.
- Build trust by adding user-generated content that allows others to chime in and confirm what you are saying, selling, or providing is useful to them.
- Predetermine the experience you want your audience to take away with them after experiencing your marketing efforts.

Networking and influence often work hand in hand. Building a solid network requires solid relationships. Take the time to listen to other people's needs so that if there comes a time when you can be influential with your resources, you will be ready and able.

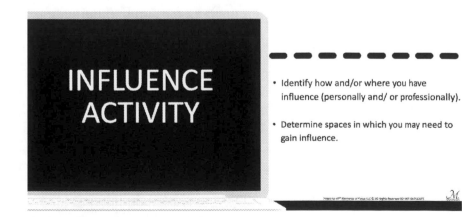

INFLUENCE ACTIVITY

- Identify how and/or where you have influence (personally and/ or professionally).

- Determine spaces in which you may need to gain influence.

Before you invest in a major networking effort, identify what influence you can offer to others and what influence you need to help you grow.

OUTSIDE INFLUENCES

In what area do you have influence? What you have to offer to your network may not come directly from you. You may work in sports but have a cousin who is a medical specialist. One of your clients or colleagues may be in dire need of a specialist. Although you are not a doctor, your access to one could be influential to someone in your network. If you have influence and can get someone an appointment with a doctor, they may be open to help you later with their access to influence.

When identifying your outside influences:

- Think of everyone in your family, friend, and business circles and outline who they are and what they do professionally.
- Highlight those who you feel may be an asset to you because you might be able to refer them to someone else in your network.
- Out of respect, call them and ask if they would be okay with you contacting them in the future to find out if you can refer them to someone in your network. This will help you be sure that you have them in your pocket to share with others as needed.
- Always let the person who is asking for the referral know that you might be able to connect them with someone who will be of help to them in case you're not able to connect them. If it works out for their benefit, they will appreciate you for using your influence to help them. If it doesn't, they will know you tried to help.

The outside influence I have access to is as follows:

_____

_____

_____

_____

_____

_____

_____

_____

_____

_____

PERSONAL INFLUENCE

- What do you have access to in your personal portfolio that can be beneficial to others?
- What have you learned, where have you traveled, and what have you experienced that can be shared?
- What have you captured along the way that would make you influential to others based on your knowledge and insight?

The personal influence I have is:

_____

_____

_____

_____

_____

_____

_____

_____

_____

_____

What influence do you need? List the areas of influence you need right now or will need in the future to meet your goals so that when people ask, "How can I help you?" you will have a short list available on the top of your head that is based on your strategic plan and may take you to your next step. For most professionals, it's easier to tell someone what they have access to share than to identify what influence they need and/or are prepared to accept.

You might say that the influence you are looking for is an executive mentor, a scholarship or grant to continue your education, or an investor based on a project that you're working on.

The influence I need as it relates to my career development is:

_____

_____

_____

_____

_____

_____

_____

_____

_____

COMMON TYPES OF NETWORKING

DEPARTMENTAL

Most people take departmental networking for granted without realizing it can have the greatest effect on immediate promotions. Because we spend so much time with our colleagues, we can form friendships that make us forget that they could be our managers someday. They might not be able to forget our work ethic or temperament. Alternatively, we might see them in the exact job that they do rather than continuously networking with them to learn more about their future plans and current business activities. If you don't network within your department, you may be surprised when you find out that the person you only knew as the clerk in your department is now the president of an organization you want to belong to.

Some companies have employees meet with their managers at the end of the year to evaluate their progress and possibly get a bonus and/or a promotion. Others require employees to go through a *360 review*. A 360 review is a process of getting feedback on an individual's performance and/or potential from their manager and others who interact with them regularly, including peers, direct reports, and managers. It is important that your brand is known and remains consistent across the board, that you develop a good rapport with everyone you work with, and that you get to know your team beyond your day-to-day work.

NETWORKING EXERCISE

Set one-on-one meetings with two people you normally work with. Disclose your areas of interests as they pertain to your industry and learn more about theirs. Discuss challenges, suggestions, and observations about your next steps. Discuss a hobby that you have in common—like golfing, basketball, or volunteer work—because people often bond over common interests.

EXECUTIVE NETWORKING

If you are invited to attend an executive team meeting—with or on behalf of your supervisor—be clear on the agenda. Find out what your expectations are for taking notes or providing a PowerPoint presentation. Listen with the intention of learning. Take a quiet yet confident posture unless you are asked to present your ideas.

If you are networking with an executive in a one-on-one meeting, remember the following:

- They are human just like you. You do not have to be intimidated by their presence. Most executives understand that young professionals are approaching them in hopes of learning and/or growing. There are many who never get approached because of their status and are happy to speak with you. When you approach them, do so with confidence and humility—and be ready to speak and learn. Ask about their thoughts about business and genuinely connect with their answers.

- Respect their time. If they give you their time, use it wisely and come with questions in hand. Some executives will give you time for an informational interview and will request your questions in advance. Be prepared to listen, take notes, and connect with their thoughts. If your time runs out before you have the opportunity to ask every question, it's okay. Make sure you ask your most important questions first—do not waste time asking questions that you can find answers to on the internet. Leave room for them to add to the conversation as they see fit.

- Ask for advice, and if it applies to your plan, do it! People don't want to feel like they are giving you incredible advice that you are not putting into practice. If they run into you later and ask if you followed up with their contact or read the book they recommended and you have not, they might not consider you a good investment of time and resources. Many people are looking for mentors, but they don't realize that sometimes before someone commits to mentoring you on a regular basis, they want to see your work ethic.

- Follow up! Send a thank-you note immediately after your meeting or call. A physical thank-you card still holds weight and adds a classy touch, but you can always send an electronic card to their email address. If they tell you to keep in touch, ask if it is okay if you follow up in a month or so to share updates. They will then tell you what works best for their schedule. Do not be offended if they don't respond right away when you follow up with them. Simply follow up later with a gentle reminder of their invitation to connect. In business, it can take six months to get a meeting. Don't get frustrated. Instead, focus on developing your professional brand in the meantime. The person who you think is going to be your mentor might never mentor you, but they may vouch for you if your name comes up in a meeting.

- Offer to help. Find out what they may need and where you might be able to serve as an asset to them.

OUTSIDE EVENTS

Whether you are at a company event, an industry conference, or a dinner, it is imperative that you represent your brand well. Be sure that you are fully aware of the purpose and mission of the event so that you know the best way to connect. This is another opportunity that requires research and being prepared to connect with purpose.

- Who is hosting the event?
- Who are the speakers?
- What is the agenda for the program?
- What companies are expected to attend?

SOCIAL MEDIA

Social media is like standing in front of an open window. When we are looking at everyone else, they can see us too—and some social media sites alert people when we are looking at their profiles. It is not a brand-development tool; it is a marketing vehicle that can be used to deliver your brand to the world.

WHAT ARE YOU MARKETING ONLINE?

 YOUR STATUS AS A ...
- Businessperson
- Commentator
- Influencer
- Writer
- Artist

 A BUSINESS

 A CAUSE/NON-PROFIT

- WHAT'S YOUR STRATEGY?

- DO YOU STAY ON BRAND?

- WHAT SERVICE OR KNOWLEDGE DO YOU PROVIDE TO YOUR AUDIENCE?

SOCIAL MEDIA EXERCISE

Log into your most frequently used social media account.

Does your social media presence, as of today, warrant an investment of time or money from others? Yes or no? Please explain:

_____

_____

_____

_____

_____

_____

_____

_____

_____

If you are currently making money from your social media presence, is there room for growth? Yes or no? Please explain:

_____

_____

_____

_____

_____

_____

_____

_____

Does your current social media presence represent the legacy that you are looking to create? Yes or no? Please explain:

_____

_____

_____

_____

_____

_____

_____

_____

_____

_____

What are the most popular social media networking sites:

_____

_____

_____

_____

_____

_____

_____

_____

_____

_____

_____

_____

_____

What was each site created for?

_____

_____

_____

_____

_____

_____

_____

_____

_____

Which works best for your brand? Why?

_____

_____

_____

_____

_____

_____

_____

_____

_____

_____

_____

Are your accounts set to private? Yes or no?

Tip: Always assume that all of your accounts are open to the public. If a company is interested in bringing you on as an employee or promoting you to become an executive, they will often look into your accounts to see what type of professional partner they are bringing on board to represent their company. Wouldn't you want to know if there was something going on with the company you were about to partner your vision with? Wouldn't you look them up and find out as much as you could? It goes both ways. They are considering who you are, how you represent yourself in public, and who you may be in partnership with.

Why are you connecting with others on social media networking sites?

_____

_____

_____

_____

_____

_____

_____

_____

_____

_____

List the number of connections you have in each of your social networks below:

_____

_____

_____

_____

_____

_____

_____

_____

How many are you leveraging for business purposes? How many can you pick up the phone and call today as a direct resource?

Your network is valuable based on your actual relationships and the access that you have to each person in your network. Since networking is the exchange of information and ideas among people with common professional or special interest, the intent is to leverage your connections for purpose. Every time you connect, ask yourself, "Why am I meeting this person—and is there a way for us to serve together in the future?"

When people I do not know invite me to connect on social media, if I feel like there is an alignment and possible strategic partnership based on their profile, I thank them and ask how they foresee us working together in the future before connecting. Most people don't actually respond until they have thought through their intent on being in touch. This often cuts out those people who just want to be connected for the sake of having another contact. It also has a way of cutting out those who really just want to align with my contacts and realize that if they are connected with me, they may be able to gain access to my network.

When I send an invitation to someone, after they accept my invitation, I send a quick note of thanks for adding me to their network and an invitation to set up a ten-minute call to learn more about their work and share information on mine in hopes of genuinely finding ways to work together in the future. As a businessperson, your time will be limited— and you'll have to make tough decisions about where to spend it. Where you invest your time is often more important than where you invest your money because if you invest your time in the right places, that investment will turn into money and opportunities.

What are the effects, the potential, and the pitfalls that can arise from utilizing social media?

_____

_____

_____

_____

_____

_____

_____

_____

FORMING STRATEGIC PARTNERSHIPS

A strategic partnership, also referred to as an alliance or joint venture, is a business partnership (usually noncompeting) that involves sharing resources between two or more individuals or companies to help all involved.

What types of partners do you have and/or are you looking to establish to grow and advance your brand? How will you utilize your partnership?

_____

_____

_____

_____

_____

_____

_____

_____

_____

_____

COWORKERS

How can you partner with the people you work with? What common goals do you have—and what resources can you share?

_____

_____

_____

_____

_____

_____

_____

_____

_____

EXECUTIVES

What might you add to the more seasoned executives in your space? What insights do you have about today's society, trends, or demographics that might serve them? What can they add to your development based on their specific background?

_____

_____

_____

_____

_____

_____

_____

_____

_____

BUSINESS PEERS

What partners in your industry have you partnered with or do you plan to partner with and why?

_____

_____

_____

_____

_____

_____

_____

_____

_____

KEY TAKEAWAYS

What am I taking away from this section on networking—and what will
I add to my networking plans?

_____

_____

_____

_____

_____

_____

_____

_____

_____

_____

_____

_____

_____

_____

_____

_____

_____

_____

_____

_____

_____

_____

PART VI

BECOMING BUSINESS SAVVY

So far, we have worked through how to discover your brand, set your expectations, and prepare for future opportunities. We have also covered techniques and systems that you can utilize to build or rebuild your brand and methods you can apply to become more effective in your networking.

I want you to focus now on becoming business savvy. Savvy typically refers to having a good understanding or practical knowledge of something. When people talk about being business savvy, they are referring to having business knowledge, insight, and expertise.

This chapter is going to concentrate on helping you build up your awareness and perspective about basic business insights that can help you maintain or advance in your position and prevent you from getting fired. Don't forget that "proper perspective brings clarity." If you have the right perspective about the situations you face, you'll see them for what they are and know how to respond accordingly. A lack of knowledge and insight can lead to becoming emotional and relying on your feelings rather than reality.

We used to give Christmas bonuses to our employees every year, but when the economy changed, we could no longer afford to provide bonuses. One of our assistants approached me in a rant, expressing her anger about not being able to depend on the Christmas bonus she had been given in the past. Unfortunately, because she didn't have the proper perspective, she wasn't clear about how she should have responded. She didn't understand that a Christmas bonus is simply extra money given by a company at their discretion and not a part of an employee's salary requirement. She also didn't realize that the shift in the economy affected our finances, and we chose to pay for the employees' health insurance for the year instead.

To gain perspective about any situation, you need to obtain knowledge and wisdom. Wisdom will help you develop understanding and good judgment. Having a great, balanced perspective will help you to see things clearly.

The following topics will help you gain great perspective as you develop:

COMPANY CULTURE

This affects everyone (executives, old and new staff, potential candidates, board members, and clients) who is connected to a company. Although company culture is often defined as a shared set of values, goals, attitudes, and practices that make up a company, every company has its own culture.

- A company's culture is typically centered around what the company produces or the services it provides as well as what the founders, owners, or senior executives value and their ideas of what constitutes an acceptable work environment. If you work with a law firm, based on the nature of your work and the expectations of your clientele, the culture may be one that is more "old school business traditional," requiring a buttoned-up suit and tie and a confidential atmosphere. A tech company may set a culture that feels open, loose, fun, and creative in an effort to promote innovation.
- Sometimes, culture refers to the attitudes and behaviors of employees and can be seen and felt in how people interact with

each other, the values they display, and the decisions they are allowed to make.

- It can also be described as friendly, hostile, customer-focused, innovative, ethical, research-driven, technology-driven, process-oriented, hierarchical, family-friendly, or risk-taking culture. Culture affects how formal, laid back, inclusive, or exclusive managers are in their leadership style.

- It is extremely important to inquire about the company culture when applying for a job. If you are interested in a larger company, ask about the culture of the department you are looking to work in since it could be slightly different based on the nature of their work. For instance, if you get hired at a movie studio, you may assume that the culture will be laid back. However, if you work in the legal department, it will not have the same vibe as being on set because the work and requirements are different. Gaining this information will help you understand how things will flow, any expectations that may be required of you, and if you will be able to adjust to or want to be a changemaker in the environment.

- Although the culture is initially set by the founders, it is carried out by the staff within the organization. This means that your behavior can have a great effect on the mood, tone, and culture of your work environment and make a difference in whether someone wants to work at your company or if clients want to stay on board. When applying for or partnering with any organization, always consider how their culture and your values align.

YOUR CURRENT POSITION

Performing well in your current job can lead to promotion. Always focus on your current job while preparing for your next position. This is a topic that gets people fired quickly. Oftentimes, when people accept a job that they feel is just a "temporary move" toward the position they really want, like an assistant, an assistant coordinator, or as assistant director, it becomes obvious to those around them that they are less concerned about their everyday tasks than on what it's going to take to get them to the next position.

RECOMMENDATIONS OF YOUR REPUTATION

The world is small, and the number of people who work in your industry is even smaller.

- If you are not planning to stay at your current company for a long period of time, understand that people across your industry are connected and will unofficially discuss your work ethic when asked. Make sure they have something great to say about your work and working with you. If your work is not great, some people, to be politically correct, won't say anything at all, which is just as bad as giving you a bad reference because they are not saying anything good. This is not about pleasing people; it is about contributing to an industry you choose to make a difference in and representing your professional brand at a consistent level across the board. Most people should have the same experience or feeling when talking about working with and/or meeting you because you should always be you.
- If you are looking to be promoted within your company, you need to know that people are always looking for the "next best talent." People are promoted all the time from one department to the next, and becoming a great asset for one team can lead to receiving an internal recommendation to another team without you even knowing it. Managers are paying attention to your skill sets, leadership traits (how you self-manage), and behavior. The skills you display for your current team may be a greater asset for another department. An opportunity to move to another department based on how you've been doing what you're doing may come with a promotion and more benefits. You never know who is watching or what position they are looking to develop around your talent. Sometimes, companies don't know they need someone like you until you show up and are able to add "little" things that provide a

little extra to the team that are aligned with their goals but had not yet been offered. You cannot just do what you want to do within your position, but you can occasionally offer suggestions that may raise the projects you are working on to the next level.

HARD WORK IS STILL RESPECTED

A lot of people respect hard work, and if they see you doing incredible work on a small job, they may go out of their way to train you or make sure you have the experience you need for where you want to go because they respect your work ethic and want to see you do well.

Although people understand that you will eventually want to be promoted, no one likes to feel used. No one likes to feel like you don't really care about the work you are doing with them. Many people believe that how you do one thing is how you will do everything. So do everything in a way that represents your integrity, values, and professional brand. Learn everything you can and meet everyone you have access to in your current space. Maximize every opportunity, leaving nothing behind except a great reputation. You never know who in your current space will meet you in the position that you are on your way to. The people you work with today may be the people you work with in the future.

When you turn in great work with time to spare, your supervisor could give or expose you to projects at the next level. When you successfully accomplish these assignments, you may then be given work at an even higher level. This is one way that people are unofficially trained for professional advancement. You will not always be paid more for these opportunities financially in the beginning, but your experience is something that will increase your earning potential over time, based on your capabilities.

You can also connect your opportunities to your professional syllabus and utilize them to upgrade your conversations in your networking circles. You can either have a perspective that leads you to say, "This is not in my job description, so I am not doing it" or "This is not in my job description, so I'm getting to learn more for my professional growth." Oftentimes, your continuous effort to produce great work will lead your supervisor to ask you what you want to do next. They may not have a promotion to offer you at the time—but never get so comfortable that you forget that you are networking with your supervisor every day. Even if they cannot help you, they may have professional contacts who can. In many cases, it doesn't make sense for your company not to promote you when you can serve as an asset at a higher level. For instance, if you are serving as my assistant, but I see that you are incredibly talented as a marketing professional, when I am ready to hire a marketing professional—since I can trust your work ethic and habits—it only benefits me to promote you to marketing and find a new assistant. This will not always happen, but in many cases, it does.

Tip: If you're looking for a promotion, always make sure that you're hitting 100 percent of your current job and show at least 30 percent of your ability to do work at the next level every day. Frequently, people are looking to be promoted, but managers and executives are looking to see if you completed your assignments successfully and if you're qualified to be given the job that you're asking to do next. They want to see qualities that assure them that you will be able to handle the job you're asking for.

Tip: Some companies will give a bonus at the end of every year that you have been with them based on what is called a year-end review. A year-end bonus in many cases is not giving you extra money; it is providing you with money for the extra work that you have been credited for that was exceptional and beyond your job description. It is not mandatory; it is given at the discretion of the company. At the end of the year, you may be evaluated on whether you exceeded, met, or didn't meet expectations. Even if there is no bonus given, a great evaluation will increase your credibility if, and, or when future opportunities arise.

INTERNAL PROMOTIONS

Work toward an internal promotion or one that you give yourself based on your professional syllabus, personal accomplishments, and professional goals. Do not wait until your supervisor evaluates your work to know where you stand. You should be evaluating yourself based on your own personal weekly reviews. If you do well, you should know it and have a record of your success for your personal notes, future conversations, and graduation into your next steps. If you had a rough year and made a lot of mistakes, it should be no surprise that you didn't receive a great review from your supervisor. You should develop a list of questions for your supervisor on a regular basis on how you can stay on track with your goals.

SMART is an acronym for *specific, measurable, achievable, realistic,* and *time-related*:

- Specific: Your goal should be a specific, well-defined, targeted area of improvement.
- Measurable: It should be measurable with specific criteria that allow you to track your progress toward the accomplishment of the goal.
- Achievable: Attainable and not impossible to achieve. Assignable: Specify who will do it and/or be attached to the necessary duties.
- Realistic: Something that is realistically within reach when provided with resources and is relevant to your life's purpose, values, dreams, and ambitions.
- Time-Related: A goal with a clearly defined timeline attached to it, including a start and targeted date of completion, such as one or six months.

Set SMART Goals

- Build a framework for your plans.
- Focus your mindset on the direction you have set out for yourself.
- Highlight where you might be challenged in your plans to help you set your strategies.

UNMOVABLE ASSETS

Make sure that you are such an asset to your team that they view you as an unmovable asset, which is someone they cannot move as successfully without. Ask yourself, "What do I—or will I—add to my team that is uniquely incredible in the process of our productivity?"

BRAND NAME PROTECTION

Professional brands are built by repetitive behavior and actions. Do what you need to do daily and be consistent in your actions to protect your brand name. Your reputation should be so strong that if someone spoke negatively against you in a way that is not reflective of who you are, no one would believe it.

EVERY DAY IS AN INTERVIEW

Every conversation you have, especially at work, is an interview. Everything you do is being evaluated. Every project you work on and action you take is part of a long, unofficial interview and is being considered when someone is contemplating how and if they might help you move forward. Be mindful of what, where, and why you make certain moves and statements. Be confident about your knowledge—and be open to learning from others. When you're great at what you do, people will be watching you to find out what opportunities they can offer you based on what you have shown or stated. When you are not great, they will be looking to find ways to make sure the work you are supposed to do gets done—perhaps by someone else.

Being business savvy is about knowing what to do. So, let's talk in general about knowing what to wear and when to wear it. Every industry, company, or organization is different, but the following are business basics for business dress codes and professional attire.

PROFESSIONAL ATTIRE

When you are invited to an interview, meeting, company event, luncheon, or dinner party, ask, "What is the attire?" In other words, "What should I wear?" It may seem like something that should be obvious, but it's not. Not all companies have the same requests when it comes to what to wear, and you should always get a clear understanding prior to attending any event. Let's take a quick look at the most common types of outfits and what you might expect others to be wearing based on the requested attire.

CASUAL ATTIRE (COMFORTABLE GEAR)

Jeans or casual pants, dresses and skirts, comfortable flats and sneakers, T-shirts, blouses, and boots—depending on the style—may all be included. Casual means different things to different companies, so always be sure to ask for clarity if you're not sure about what is expected. Find the balance between casual and too casual. If your supervisor invites you to a BBQ at their home, remember that this is still a work event for you. If you wear shorts, perhaps pair them with a shirt with a collar. Don't wear anything that is too short or revealing because you are still at a work event. If you are going to an office team retreat in the mountains, know that it's just as inappropriate to be overdressed for a casual work event as it is to be underdressed. The idea is to be appropriate for the event and the tasks that are planned. If your team will be hiking, and you have on dress shoes, you will not be able to participate—or you might become the topic of conversation and a distraction from the planned team-bonding experience.

BUSINESS CASUAL (EVERYDAY COMMON OFFICE WEAR)

A nice pair of khakis, dress pants, blouses, shirts with collars, dress shoes, loafers, skirts, professional dresses, and sweaters. Neckties are usually optional.

SMART CASUAL (DRESSIER, STYLISH CASUAL)

Often considered a chic, put-together ensemble. Various definitions apply, depending on the company, but in general, smart casual requires a balance between a polished office look, including a blazer, business shoes, a nice belt, and informal clothes like a crisp, dark pair of jeans, a casual dress, or a high-end T-shirt to create a relaxed style that appears effortlessly tailored, comfortable, and neat.

BUSINESS PROFESSIONAL (TRADITIONAL BUSINESS WEAR)

A suit or slacks, sports jacket and tie, or a dress with dress shoes. Business professional is the "traditional" way of dressing for work. The expectations of business professional are the most standardized and generally the same: pantsuits or skirt suits, matching jackets and pants or skirts with button-down shirts, a necktie, and black or brown dress shoes.

SEMIFORMAL

Attire often requested at semiformal occasions such as holiday parties, weddings, and dinner events. It is similar to business professional, but it is less formal than a cocktail party outfit. Options include button-down shirts, dress pants, dress shoes, dresses, and loafers, and a dark suit is always a good option. If you choose to wear a suit, a tie or bowtie is optional. A blazer or sports coat is suitable for during the day, and a suit jacket works for evening events. This category also includes midi dresses, maxi dresses, wrap dresses, cocktail dresses, pantsuits, and jumpsuits. Heels, sandals, flats, and dress shoes are appropriate choices for semiformal events, depending on location.

FORMAL/BLACK TIE/BLACK TIE OPTIONAL

A conservative dress code reserved for formal events. Dressy attire, tuxedos, black suits, white shirts, floor-length dresses, or ball gowns.

Tip: If you obtain a new job and need to go shopping for new outfits, I suggest that if you're not 100 percent certain on the office vibe, buy a few basic pieces based on what you have been told about the office dress code. Wear them for the first few days and pay attention to what others are wearing so that you can get a true sense of the office standards. Then, go buy your other items that fall within the dress code but reflect your personal style.

Tip: Something as simple as ironing clothes is seen as an investment of personal care, awareness, and self-confidence. When you do not iron your clothes, it can send a sign to others that you are not concerned enough about yourself to invest time into your self-care. It may be assumed that you are a "do things at the last minute" type of person who jumps out of bed, grabs what they can find, and runs out the door. People may think that this mindset is how you may process your work.

BUSINESS ETIQUETTE

Following common office guidelines can help you develop the proper perspective to advance in and gain the most from your opportunities. A lack of understanding in these areas might hinder your progression.

OPPORTUNITY VERSUS OBLIGATION

The words that you use to describe the options that you have will affect your perspective and your behavior. Although we're provided with opportunities, there are no obligations that require us to go to work. We don't "have to" work; we "get to" work. There's a great benefit for those who are able to serve, especially within an industry of choice. Being able to train for a position in your industry of choice is a great opportunity. It's also a chance to accomplish items on your professional syllabus. If the only job you can get for now is not in your preferred industry, it may still help you build the skills for the job you want. It could simply provide you with the money you need while you are in another educational environment (having a job during school or working in your dream office to gain experience without earning enough to maintain your expenses).

Many people feel that if they were rich, they would never look at work as an opportunity. Most people, however, even the richest ones, eventually want an opportunity to do something productive with their lives—even if its time spent donating to others. Participating in charity events still requires a level of organization, knowledge, work, skills, and support. Set your mind to acknowledge the benefits you have access to that will help you in whatever your professional goals are.

EDUCATION IS KEY

Being in a work environment exposes you to the norms of the business structure of your industry and allows you to grow.

THE WORK ENVIRONMENT (OFFICE, MOVIE SET, ART STUDIO, FOOTBALL FIELD)

Industries are different across the board—and so are the physical and cultural work environments. When I work with football players, I have to adjust to their environment since it is different than my clients who are film directors or corporate officers. I have had to learn how to maneuver in each environment while staying true to my brand—and you will too.

PERSONAL GROWTH

Go into your opportunities with an expectation of learning about the job, the work environment, and yourself. Pay attention to how your exposure and experience are growing you forward. Take the time to step back weekly and assess how you feel about what you have accomplished based on your projects, conversations, and actions and how you can do better. There is nothing like watching an episode of your own life, especially when you have time to make improvements in real time.

As a young professional, you may be handed what appear to be mundane, ordinary, monotonous assignments that seem useless for your growth. I am going to share examples that can help you develop your mind and maximize opportunities by recognizing the benefits attached to any situation.

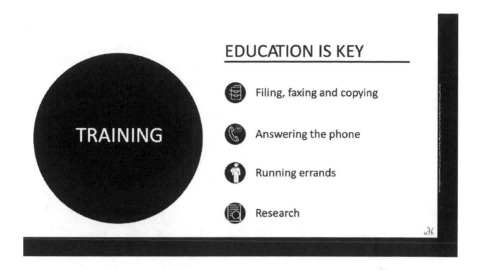

EDUCATION IS KEY

- Filing, faxing and copying
- Answering the phone
- Running errands
- Research

TRAINING

FILING, FAXING, AND COPYING

Having the opportunity to file, fax and/or copy documents is a great part of your research and development. Of course, there are documents that you will not be given permission to read, and it is understood that everything you view is confidential and cannot be copied or shared with anyone, including coworkers. This learning experience provides you with knowledge of what business documents look like in your industry.

ANSWERING THE PHONE

When you are answering the phone, you should be paying close attention to who's calling so that you can become familiar with the players in the game of your business. You should be connecting who they are to what you are learning along the way. I have seen many receptionists and assistants get promotions based on the experiences they provided to the clients and how efficient their work was. I have also seen clients come into the office and want to meet and get to know more about the person who is always professional and exceptional with client and/or customer care. This is not about looking for the next job from someone you speak with on the phone; it is about developing great rapport with people in your industry.

RUNNING ERRANDS

The benefit of running errands or delivering packages across a corporate campus or studio lot is that it allows you to get to know who the players in your company are and where their offices are located. It also allows you to say hello and put a name to a face. Although it's not an opportunity to have meetings with them or disrupt their work, most people will say hello, ask your name, and introduce themselves. This is another opportunity to display professionalism and your brand.

DOING RESEARCH

Sometimes, depending on your industry, you may be asked to do extensive research for your department. Although it may not seem fun or creative, you are being asked to research information in an industry that you want to be in at a very high level for real-case scenarios. Essentially, they are paying you to learn and develop.

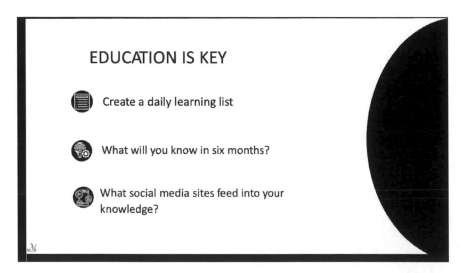

CREATE A DAILY LEARNING LIST

After you have developed your professional syllabus, create a list of what you can learn from your job. Look for opportunities to learn as much as you can every day. For instance, you may list that you need to learn how to create a company portfolio and use a specific social media platform for business purposes. Even though the manager or executive you support may not have time to teach you on a regular basis, because these items are on your list, you will be looking for chances to learn more as opportunities come. If there is quiet time in a casual conversation or an official meeting, and you are asked what you'd like to learn or how they can help you, you will have a mental list to pull from. As you are given assignments, you will be able to check off certain things on your list.

WHAT WILL YOU KNOW IN SIX MONTHS?

Every six months, you should ask yourself, "What will I know and how will I have grown in six months?" This will give you a short-term road map based on your big-picture goals. How will I be different? What will I be working on? Sometimes your job will not change over a six-month period, but your knowledge and professional experiences can. Within six months, you may plan to attend a professional conference or network with specific colleagues.

WHAT SOCIAL MEDIA SITES FEED INTO YOUR KNOWLEDGE?

What networking sites do you intentionally use to learn from? Which do you utilize to find news about what's happening in your industry? It is imperative that you are up to speed with what's happening in your field so that you can make your plans for your career, contribute to conversations in your professional circle, and develop thoughts and strategies that can help move things forward in your industry. Many people learn how to speak English by watching TV. You learn by listening and gaining an understanding, and as you are learning the language of your business at a higher level, be sure to tap into articles and online conversations from trusted sources.

EDUCATION IS KEY

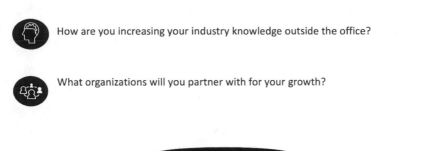

How are you increasing your industry knowledge outside the office?

What organizations will you partner with for your growth?

GROWTH

HOW ARE YOU INCREASING YOUR INDUSTRY KNOWLEDGE OUTSIDE OF THE OFFICE?

It is easy to get comfortable depending solely on your company for training and development, especially when you work within a wonderful organization that offers in-house resources. I have heard many people say, "My company will teach me what I need to know" or "I will have access to it when I'm ready." Whether your company is providing opportunities or not, it's important to look for outside resources for growth, including classes, one-on-one networking opportunities, conferences, workshops, and organizations.

WHAT ORGANIZATIONS WILL YOU PARTNER WITH?

Develop organization affiliations. Joining incredible organizations that are aligned with your professional goals can serve as a major asset for your career development. They allow you to join a community of people who share your interests and provide local and national learning and networking opportunities. I have seen cases where two people are applying for the same job. They have the same levels of talent, skill, and experience, but one is an active member of a national organization that represents their industry. In one case, the candidate with the organization affiliation was selected based on their networking power. Because they had access to an organization with thirty thousand members—who they could pull from their network for the benefit of what the company was producing—they were deemed a better professional partner.

What to Look For

- Local and national networking opportunities: If possible, you want to look for organizations with local, national, and international chapters. This will allow you to participate at the local level and connect with other people at the national and international levels. At a national conference for engineers, there were thousands of engineers who were all affiliated with this network. There were so many opportunities to have conversations with engineers from across the country at conference events, the hotel, and restaurants.
- Extended educational opportunities: When you join an organization, you are looking for extended learning opportunities. Most organizations have workshops, seminars, panel discussions, and events that provide education for their members. You want to join so that you can be connected to what's happening now and be in the rooms with the thought leaders who are discussing what's set to happen in the future. You can apply what you learn to your career planning and use the information to be an asset to your company.
- Additional leadership opportunities: Once you join, you don't want to just be an audience member. You want to look for additional opportunities that allow you to grow and share with the professionals who are coming right behind you. Once you get in, find out how you can become a committee member, sit on a panel, participate in facilitating a workshop, and grow within your industry by being a leader in your organization. Be sure to position yourself to eventually be able to give back to the organizations that have given to you.
- Professional mentors and sponsors: One of the great things about being a member of an organization is the potential for developing relationships with people who can serve as professional mentors

or sponsors. You are looking for people who, based on their knowledge of who you are and trust in your brand—as well as their relationship with you—are willing to help pull you up within your industry. During your time with your mentor or sponsor, you should expect to grow by utilizing the benefits of having a guide at your side. These are not "everyday relationships." You should not expect to talk to your mentor or sponsor every day. Typically, they will meet with you to learn more about what you are looking to accomplish, help you set a road map and goals, and give you suggestions for what you can do next. After you show that you have completed their suggested assignment or the goals you stated you would complete, they may set a time to discuss your next steps.

- Be flexible in your understanding of scheduling time as it pertains to meeting with anyone who offers to serve as an advisor in your life. They generally have extremely busy schedules, but they are volunteering their time to help you. Some mentors will set up weekly, monthly, or quarterly meetings to check on your progress, depending on their schedules. Meetings are usually set for an hour unless you have scheduled a quick check-in. Let them set the terms for your meetings because they may only have time for ten-minute calls.
- Always maximize the time you have with a business coach, mentor, sponsor, or advisor. Come with an agenda for your meeting.
- Make sure you address the most important issues first in case they have to cut your meeting short.
- Be prepared to share important updates that showcase your progress.
- Always ask for advice on next steps.

Professional affiliations add additional perks to your resume and bio:

- They show that you're not just interested in a job but are seriously invested in the industry.
- They provide opportunities to increase your knowledge and leadership experience.
- They increase the access to people that your company may want to partner with.

HOW TO FIND ORGANIZATIONS

- Online research: Look up National Society/Association of … (fill in the blank).
- Contact the human resources departments at your company and/or at large corporations that are affiliated with your profession and ask which organizations they support and recommend.
- Ask senior-level employees which organizations they belong to and serve in.

Tip: If you cannot afford the regular professional membership, ask about young professional discount rates, scholarships, and volunteer opportunities.

EVERYONE CANNOT MAKE THE TEAM

- Each team, job, and opportunity is not for everyone.
- Opportunities are typically about skill sets, experience, personality, and the culture surrounding the position. If you do not get selected for a position that you apply for, take the time to measure any areas that you may need to grow in so that you can learn from the experience and move toward success.
- You might be considered just as qualified as the next candidate as it pertains to your skills and experience, but your personality may not fit into the culture of the organization. I worked in an office where the language was really rough, and although the company met candidates who were "qualified" based on their skills, they were not a "good fit" for the position based on the personalities of the staff in the office and the office culture. I also remember a candidate who had fifty years of experience but took herself out of the hiring process because the office culture required that the employees worked until 11:00 p.m. or midnight on a regular basis, which did not work well for her. There are more than one or two reasons why people don't get selected for a team, *and* there may be reasons why you are not interested in a job or promotion. It's important to assess your desires and plans and be honest with yourself and your team. Remember that companies want their

employees to be happy serving in their positions since it keeps up the morale and adds to their overall success. You want to find a team that works well for who you are and is a great fit. Oftentimes, the best way to know what works best for you is through exposure and experience. Don't shy away from an offer because it does not seem to be the best fit. Take the time to evaluate all the areas of your plan when considering an offer.

Find the right opportunities. It may take time, but it's important to look for opportunities that work for you.

What culture do you feel like you'll thrive in? How can you best utilize your skills on a team?

_____

_____

_____

_____

_____

_____

_____

_____

_____

_____

GO HARD OR GO HOME

This expression was common years ago when people would work on a job and get paid at the end of the day based on the success of their work. "Work hard with us while we get this job done or go home because you're hindering us from what we're looking to accomplish." Always keep in mind that you're working on a team and that people are counting on you to get your work done. Try to consider several things as you focus on your work habits.

DON'T RELAX YOUR STANDARDS

You may find that you are working in an office where people relax to a point that they don't get their work done on a regular basis. That might even become the office standard. However, you have to remember that you are building your professional brand and are not going to work at the level that other people set for themselves. Work at the level that you expect of yourself. Of course, there'll be times when everybody will take breaks, relax, or maybe even have parties, and that is normal. There may also be times when you can't finish your work because someone else has not given you what you need to complete it. This idea is not about you being a robot, and you will have to adjust to office standards to some degree. Don't relax your work habits or work ethic just because others do.

MAKE PEOPLE FORGET YOU'RE IN TRAINING

As a young professional, regardless of what your title is, you want to make your team feel as though you're a core part of the team. You want them to feel like your work is blending right in with the level of work that the company is producing. You do not want them to see you as a "young professional" but as a general member of the team.

WORK LIKE YOU HAVE THE JOB YOU WANT

Don't wait to get promoted to showcase your work habits and work ethic at the level that you want to be promoted to. People want to see if you're capable of doing the job that you're interested in. The moment that you state an interest, they begin to consider if they feel confident enough to refer you for the position or promotion. Make sure that you work at the level for the job that you want. People often say, "I always knew that they would wind up being in a position like that because their skill set, work ethic, mannerisms, and leadership have always been there—even when they were working in the position that they had prior to this one."

WORK AS IF IT COULD BE YOUR LAST DAY

Leave a great lasting impression every day. Nothing's guaranteed. A company could be forced to make changes and lay off their team with no notice. If there are sudden changes within your company, make sure you can walk away with a letter of recommendation that can be used for your next step.

MAKE YOURSELF AN UNMOVABLE ASSET

Make sure that people understand the need for the work that you do. Others should be able to recognize the impact you have on your company's workflow or product. When you are able to display who you are as a teammate and how valuable you are to the team, you can sometimes put yourself in a position to become an unmovable asset (someone they never want to replace). Based on the benefit you add to the productivity of the team, people will occasionally petition to keep you on in a tough situation. Develop such a great work ethic that you become a part of the machine that moves the work forward productively.

PROTECT YOUR BRAND NAME

Make sure that you are protecting what you've taken so much time to invest in with what you say, what you do, and how you do it. Your brand name should be so set that people only connect your first and last name to what you built to be your brand.

BE PREPARED FOR OPPORTUNITIES AS THEY COME BY DEVELOPING A TEAMMATE MINDSET

It's important to prepare yourself as a team player and stay aware of what is happening around you. Position yourself like a basketball player who sits on the bench and doesn't play in the game at the level of the all-stars but knows the plays, has trained and practiced beyond belief, and is always ready to run into the game in case one of the star players gets hurt. I've seen people who were working in one capacity, and then an employee got hurt or had a baby, and that position immediately became open. Many companies want to hire from within, and if you are qualified and have paid attention to what a newly vacant position requires, it could put you in a better position for a job offer before the position gets listed to the public because you're already in the company's system, are familiar with the culture, and know how to do the job. In some cases, it makes it easier to transition or promote you than to find someone from the outside. Make sure you take the time to pay attention to the requirements of the work that is happening around you.

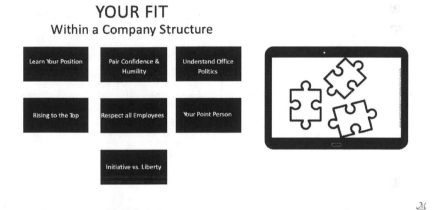

YOUR FIT
Within a Company Structure

Learn Your Position	Pair Confidence & Humility	Understand Office Politics
Rising to the Top	Respect all Employees	Your Point Person
Initiative vs. Liberty		

- Study your job description. Fully understand what the expectations are and what you need to do in order to excel.
- Gain a good understanding of how your position fits within your company structure. Learn how your work partners with the work of the departments around you.
- Be clear about the effect and impact your contributions have on the company's success. What are the results that will come from your work—and how will the results influence the company?

Tip: A quick way to realize how your work will impact your company is to ask yourself what would happen if your position didn't exist.

Be careful how you rise to the top. Many people rise to the top because of their relationships. They get hooked up, shown favor, or are connected to positions or promotions because someone is helping them get to the next level. Having an advantage can be a great thing, but you have to know how to move forward when you are given a golden ticket.

When you have not gone through the normal process of climbing to the top, it is easy to forget that other people have. Stay aware of the traditional pathways that most people are required to take to get to where you are—or where you are going—so that you maintain a balanced and humble mindset.

Be really careful because if you are stepping on people's heads to get to the top, and they wind up being there before you arrive, it could be problematic for you.

Treat other people with respect and dignity—no matter their position. Unfortunately, it is common for people to belittle others or treat them terribly when they do not see them as being useful to their advancement or when they believe that whoever hooked them up will protect them from bad behavior. People are always watching, discussing, and noting your actions. Make sure you give them something great to talk about. The person who brought you in could quit, get fired, or die. If that happens, and their favor was the only thing keeping you there, you may be asked to leave as well, especially if you have not shown and proven why you're an asset.

PAIR CONFIDENCE AND HUMILITY

Always pair your confidence with humility. As a company representative, you need to be confident about what you are presenting to the company for its benefit. You also need to be humble enough to learn and accept whatever changes are implemented along the way.

UNDERSTAND OFFICE POLITICS

Politics is associated with the set of activities that are connected to making powerful decisions in groups, such as the distribution of resources or status. Every company has some form of office politics, activities that are associated with making decisions in groups, especially when dealing with who gets what resources and status. Although you may not be able to change the office politics in your company, it is important that you observe and are aware of what they are so that you do not get stuck in a bad situation.

Organizational politics are informal, unofficial, and sometimes behind-the-scenes efforts to sell ideas, influence an organization, increase power, or achieve other targeted objectives (Brandon and Seldman 2004; Hochwarter, Witt, and Kacmar 2000). Office politics are typically seen as negative, based on the antics people use to get what they want. However, when people use these efforts to come together for the good of everyone, it can bring forth positive change within an organization. Most commonly, office politics refers to employees using their authority or power for a personal agenda.

Individuals and groups within a company may disagree about how resources (money, staff, or supplies) should be allocated, wanting them for themselves or their teams. They might align with other like-minded people to find out-of-the box ways to get what they want. They might bypass the typical rules or chain of command that everyone else is asked to follow to gain special favors, promotions, or projects. It can create jealousy, resentment, and low morale for those who are not willing to push their agendas forward in this manner.

RESPECT ALL EMPLOYEES

Never walk into a company arrogantly, treating people as though you are better than them because of the title you carry or the position they have. You never know who someone really is (their background and/experience), how they got their job (who they may be connected to), or why they chose to take it (they may be creating leverage for their next move, taking an intentional moment to slow down, or genuinely love supporting others in your industry).

A receptionist is often considered a basic, starter position. There are a lot of assumptions about why someone is in that position. People may assume that they are not smart or trained enough to do anything else or don't have any connections to help them along their way. Don't make assumptions. They may be using the job to make money while they are secretly getting a degree, planning to work their way up in the company, or just really liking the job. Respect and network with your coworkers across the board.

KNOW THE DIFFERENCE BETWEEN INITIATIVE AND LIBERTY

There is a huge difference between taking initiative and taking liberties. When someone gives you a job and tells you that you have permission or the authority to take some initiative within your position, you need to be very clear about what they mean and ask about your boundaries.

Initiative refers to having permission to stretch within the bounds of your job description. Your job description is like a box. Unless you are told otherwise, you are expected to stay within the frame of that box. When you are told that you can take the initiative, it often means that you can color within the box of your position. You can use markers, crayons, colored pencils, and glitter—as long as you stay within that box. Once you have done a great job showing initiative within that box, people might expand the box a bit, allowing you to stretch and take the initiative within a bigger box.

Initiative does not mean liberty. Liberty means freedom. Unless you are told otherwise or own your company, you do not have permission to do whatever you want to do outside of your job description.

It's like an assistant whose job it is to take notes for the CEO during the weekly meeting deciding to put together a full presentation about what he believes will be a great plan for the CEO to present. As a part of his job, he can suggest a more elevated presentation platform or updated slide deck, but it's not within his position to tell the CEO what he believes he should be presenting unless he is asked.

Tip: Before you offer suggestions, ask questions. If you have great suggestions that you want to present and have developed a rapport with your manager, always find out more about the company's current plans and/or history around the idea. You might find out that what you are suggesting is in the works or is not being considered because it has failed in the past.

KNOW YOUR POINT PERSON

When you start a new job, be clear about who your immediate supervisor will be and be aware of those in the office who can help you in times of need. Depending on how your company is structured, the person your work is most beneficial to might not be the person you report to. You may make marketing materials for the chief marketing officer but never actually meet with that officer. Rather, your instructions may come directly from the vice president of marketing. You may report directly to the VP of marketing, but that may not be who you are going to run to when you need marketing materials or office supplies. It may be the office manager or the receptionist. In any position, you want to know who your immediate supervisor is, who your work is supporting, and who you can go to for small favors around the office.

	Focus on Your Assignments		
DAILY STRATEGY	BE ABOUT YOUR BUSINESS	TOO GOOD VS. TOO BUSY	RUMORS, POLITICS, AND DRAMA

FOCUS ON YOUR ASSIGNMENTS

- When you go to the office, you should have a strategy on how you are going to spend your day and accomplish your goals. Know what's on the priority and execution list for your team and prepare a game plan that focuses on:
  - your team's mission for the day

- your expected contribution
- your plans for a successful delivery or execution of your work

- Questions to ask yourself daily:
  - What is my mission for the day?
  - What are my goals to meet my mission?
  - What tasks need to be completed to meet those goals?
  - What is my timeline for each task?

- Even on days when the office workflow is slow, have a backup project in mind. If you do not have any work due, ask yourself:
  - How can I prepare or organize for the next project?
  - Is there anything I can research now to give my team an advantage moving forward?
  - Could another team member use my support?

Tip: Check with your manager in advance about their protocol for supporting other team members. Find out if it is okay and who you have the authorization to work with when they have no work for you to do.

BE ABOUT YOUR BUSINESS

One of the ways to alleviate personal drama in the office is to be known as someone who is focused on their assignments and business at hand.

TOO GOOD VERSUS TOO BUSY

A company can be like a professional playground that is full of the same personalities and behaviors that you have experienced in high school. Don't be surprised when you witness office gossip, rumors, or drama. When you're working around people who like to gossip or are not as focused as you are on their work, it's important not to come across as someone who has the type of attitude that you are better than your coworkers. To avoid this, it becomes best practice in these scenarios to seem as though you are not engaging because you are busy with your work.

When you are asked to hang out and join a conversation but can detect that it's not somewhere you should be, you can always smile and say, "I actually have to work on this project or do some research, but I'll see you all later." That way, you don't have the problems that come with people thinking that you're too good to connect with them in the office when you just want to focus on not being caught up in the drama or delaying your productivity.

RUMORS, POLITICS, AND DRAMA

Never get involved in rumors, politics, or drama. Whenever you are talking with people, there is generally an emotional effect associated with what you say and how they feel based on what they already believe or have experienced.

If you get swept into a negative conversation or one forms around you that you cannot move away from (because it is happening in front of your workspace), be mindful and intentional about what you say since it might be quoted or misquoted. Even if your manager is leading the conversation, do not add anything negative to the conversation. The world is small, and when you're talking about somebody else's situation, you never know:

- who is connected to that person
- how people may align your response with who they think you are as a person
- how someone may think that you're judging them because they are secretly doing the same thing and you are completely unaware

A TV actress has been in the news for cheating on her husband. Because everybody in the office is talking about the drama like it's a movie and you don't think you'll ever meet that person, you may feel like chiming into the conversation.

However, two things can occur:

- Your boss might actually be related to that celebrity and may develop a dislike for you because you're someone who gossips.
- You may agree with the celebrity's decision to cheat on her husband but not know that your boss's husband just cheated on her. Although it's not the same story, your boss may develop a dislike for you because she connects what you're saying to what happened to her. She might judge you as hard as she judges the person who cheated on her.

Everything you say matters. Getting involved in rumors and drama will not help your professional reputation in the long run.

STAY AWAY FROM POLITICAL CONVERSATIONS

Unless you actually work in politics, avoid sharing who you voted for and your political views in the office. People get very heated and tend to cast personal judgments of how smart, decent, kind, sane, and trustworthy their coworkers are based on who and what they vote for. When asked, you can always calmly express that you prefer not to get into conversations about your views on politics. This implies that you have views that you stand for but would rather talk about something else.

BOREDOM

Never complain about being bored. Being bored demonstrates that you have no initiative, vision, or self-leadership. If you run out of work to do:

- Reach out to your manager and let them know that you have finished all the projects that have been assigned to you and that you want to know what else they'd like for you to accomplish.
- If they have nothing else for you to do, ask if you can work on a project, based on a need you see around the office.
- If there are no tasks, find out if you can support anybody else in the company or department. Some managers will allow you to reach out, which will increase your networking and cross-training

abilities, but others will not. The decision typically has to do with what the company or your department sets as standard and can be based on various reasons.

- If there is no one to ask or support, look at your list of things you could be reading or researching for your personal development and the development of your team.

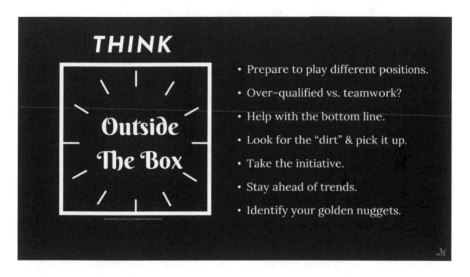

THINK OUTSIDE THE BOX

This refers to navigating forward outside of standardized thinking. This phrase is linked to doing tasks that are not within the box of your job description but are still beneficial to your company. For the sake of this conversation, we're going to focus on a few out of the box topics to consider when adding to your team.

PREPARE TO PLAY DIFFERENT POSITIONS

As much as possible, make sure that you are prepared to play different positions on your team so that you are agile enough to be an asset at every level. Even if you're not taking on an actual job in another position, you should have enough knowledge to be able to contribute, if asked, to other projects, conversations, and tasks in your organization. Being prepared comes from:

- studying what your company is doing
- paying attention to what is happening around you
- networking and learning more about what your colleagues are working on
- understanding how all the company's positions work together

BEING OVERQUALIFIED VERSUS TEAMWORK

It's necessary to understand the difference between being overqualified for a job and being a team player. Although you wouldn't normally accept a job working eight hours a day on projects that you are overqualified for, sometimes it's necessary to assist on a project that requires that everyone's hands are on deck. Your organization needs the support of everyone, at every level, to push through and finish a major project. A doctor would not serve as a nurse on an everyday basis, but in an emergency situation, they would perform the duties as needed.

A lot of people say, "I cannot do that. I'm overqualified for that." If you're being asked to do something that is not in your job description on an everyday basis, it's definitely a conversation that can be brought up with your manager for clarity in the future. If your company needs you to add to the team in a different capacity occasionally, you have to consider the big picture.

HELP WITH THE BOTTOM LINE

In business, the bottom line refers to the company's profit. Sometimes it's just a matter of helping the team get to the finish line. This may involve supporting people and projects outside of your immediate team when there's a need.

LOOK FOR THE DIRT—AND PICK IT UP

None of us want to do the dirty work. Most people prefer to take on an executive mindset and only work on projects that are at a very high level.

Being willing to organize something as small as the break room, the conference room, or the kitchen when you have nothing to do matters, especially when an organization is in the thick of the work. I have seen executive assistants and coordinators get promoted based on the little things that they do on a consistent basis in the most stressful moments. Their efforts to make sure that everything in their department was organized because there was so much chaos in a project showed initiative and foresight. Having an organized environment helps teams focus and see through the chaos to their goals. Many executives would organize things themselves if they had the time just to keep their minds clear.

Tip: This does not mean that you take on organizing the office on a regular basis if it's out of your job description. It means that you do your job at an extremely high level and contribute, when possible, to help the team.

STAY AHEAD OF TRENDS

Being in the know or having insight into what's happening in your industry can be extremely beneficial to you and your company. When you are doing your research and development and studying items surrounding your goals, company, and industry, you will never know how or when you can utilize what you know. A news article on an industry that I work in popped up on one of my social media feeds, which I thought was interesting. What I didn't know was that what was in that article would be an important fact that I would share in two meetings with two clients over the next two days. That information wound up serving as a major asset to moving our work forward.

As you are studying to learn more about what's happening in your industry, remember that what you are learning will probably be something that you will eventually share with others. You might end up saying, "I just read an article that reported that _____ company is coming out with

_____ product line, which could mean _____ for the project that we're working on." Always try to stay ahead of what's happening so that you can contribute accordingly.

IDENTIFY YOUR GOLDEN NUGGETS

What are the great skill sets, talents, and/or leadership traits that you would consider your golden nuggets? One of my golden nuggets is my ability to listen to and assess circumstances at an extremely high level, which allows me to help create companies and models with my clients through their vision. What are the special things that you can add to a project or offer to a team?

My golden nuggets are:

_____

_____

_____

_____

_____

_____

_____

_____

_____

_____

MANEUVERING WORKPLACE RELATIONSHIPS

All relationships have challenges, and most have benefits, but developing relationships within the workplace requires a specific level of intent, an understanding of people, and forethought.

- Networking: Don't forget to network at your office. Networking allows you to foster relationships with others that are mutually beneficial to the careers of you and those in your network.
- Operational networking: Building relationships within your company to get work done.
- Strategic networking: Recruiting the support of people who can help you accomplish your strategic business goals.
- Professional networking: Building relationships with other professionals both in your field and in other related fields.
- Cross-departmental networking: Cross-departmental communication happens when employees from separate departments within a company like finance, operations, marketing, and/or human resources communicate in an effort to work together on a company goal across team lines. The relationships that you build across various departments will increase your ability to get the input you'll need to get your work done.

WHO SHOULD YOU NETWORK WITH?

Network with as many people within your company as possible. When an executive starts a new job, they often schedule time in the first few months for quick meetings with as many people as possible to develop strategic partnerships with the people who work within the company.

They want to know:

- more about the people they will be working with (how their positions play into the success of the company and what they are interested in)
- what they are currently working on
- how they might work together in the future

Tip: Developing engaging relationships and an open door for communication among your coworkers can increase your ability to build your network. Your interactions will teach you more about the company or industry and may open doors into your network's network.

INFORMATION TO SHARE?

When providing information about yourself at work, be mindful about what information you share. Give people information that helps them get to know why you are someone they should get to know and be connected to. Try to share your professional background, interests, goals, mission, and vision.

KEEP YOUR MEETINGS PROFESSIONAL

No one wants to work with a robot. Therefore, people will ask personal questions to help them feel like they know you personally and not just as a coworker.

It's your job from day one to decide what type of information you want shared and how and why you are sharing it. What you say can be taken out of context or be used against you later, so be extremely intentional about the doors you open into certain areas of your life. Always assume that everything you say will be repeated and that there are no secrets at work. Just like with other relationships, everything is good—until it's not. Be prepared to answer common questions: Where are you from? Where do you live? Are you married? Where do your parents live? Do you have siblings or children?

Decide if and how much you want everyone to know and share only that. You want to come across as a balanced person, but you're not obligated to give your full history about your personal life to your coworkers. Until you feel comfortable, try to focus on activities that have to do with your field, like participating in organizations or traveling to conferences. When building your brand name, make sure that when you have time to speak to others, you leave them with a good feeling and the information that you need them to have.

Tip: Don't be upset when people make assumptions about your personal life based on what you or your family post publicly. Make sure that what you share at work is consistent with what you share online.

WHERE SHOULD YOU NETWORK WITH YOUR COWORKERS?

For general meetings, meet your coworkers for breakfast or lunch. Schedule meetings in public places to alleviate any sort of misunderstandings. If you have to take clients to dinner meetings, make sure you are in a well-trafficked public location. Sometimes people will ask you to go to dinner, but they're really asking you on a date. Reserve dinners for group meetings when possible.

Pay attention to social cues without coming across as panicked or accusatory—and always come with an agenda. Your agenda might be to get to know each other better or talk about a project. So, be clear and ask yourself, "Why am I utilizing this time for this moment?" Many people, depending on their industry, network at ball games, and some companies set up networking events at bowling alleys. For one-on-one meetings, try to set up at a location that will allow you both to hear each other talk.

ASSOCIATIONS

When you start a new position, don't become best friends with anyone until you are able to do your own personal assessment of your coworkers' behavior, reputation, and work ethics. Be cordial with everyone starting on day one, but when you walk into an office, you don't know the people you're working with. If you are immediately drawn to and become best friends with the person in the office who everyone knows as the company liar, they may think you are just like them because you gravitated to them so quickly. Take the time to get to know who's there because birds of a feather *do* flock together. It is often assumed that whoever you're close to on a regular basis is someone you have a lot of commonalities with. Get to know people before you connect with them on a close level.

DATING IN THE WORKPLACE

Many companies have a no-dating policy because relationships don't always last. Be sure to check your employee handbook for your company's standards. If you're dating somebody in the office and break up, it creates tension for everybody else. It also puts the company at risk of losing an employee because one person may not want to see the person who they're no longer interested in dating on an everyday basis. It's best not to date people you work with. I always advise people not to combine their career, money, and emotions because—although there are always exceptions to rules—it usually doesn't play out well.

PUBLIC KNOWLEDGE OF PERSONAL CHALLENGES

Don't get into the habit of telling people at work what your personal challenges are because it could come back to be a problem in the long run. One of your friends at work may get promoted and then have an opportunity to promote you to work on their team. They may not, however, be able to promote you in good conscience based on what you have told them about your personal matters.

I have heard people say these things behind closed doors:

- "I really want to hire him, but I know that he can't manage his own money. I don't feel comfortable with him managing the company's money while on a team that I am responsible for."
- "I don't think this is the right time to promote her because she's having a lot of problems at home, and it may interfere with her focus on this project."

People will sympathize with you when you're having problems at home with parents, siblings, or a spouse because they are human and can truly understand. However, when they are put into a leadership position—where your behavior can affect the projects they are responsible for—they cannot unhear what they've heard. They may have to consider it when making decisions.

MANAGING FRIENDS

Be very careful with friendships in the workplace because once you start to excel, it can be hard to manage your friends. People who work closely with you at work should not be surprised if you become their team manager. Based on the great work that you do, it should be expected that you will eventually get a promotion. Make sure that you position yourself so that if you become your friend's new manager, they will already be familiar with the standards and expectations that you have for your work and will want to support your success.

Tip: If you are working side by side with someone who you have developed a friendship with and they get promoted to be your manager, it is your responsibility to recognize the new boundaries that may need to be set in place. Certain changes or guidelines may be part of their new position. Don't make it hard for them to give you advice or guidance.

Time management will add balance to who you are personally and professionally:

- Always know what time you're supposed to be at work—and make sure you're there at least fifteen minutes early. There's an old saying that many executives still set their expectations by: "You're on time if you're at work fifteen minutes early and late if you're on time." That expression is beneficial because studies show that you're more relaxed, prepared, and motivated when you're early.
- If your organization doesn't open the doors early to allow you inside, arrive early so that you're not caught in last-minute traffic.
- If they allow you to come into your office early, take the time to come in and get settled. If you need to prepare your notes for the day, get adjusted in the bathroom, or get something out of the kitchen, use that time to get organized.
- If you are supposed to be at work at nine o'clock, make sure you're not eating, catching up with friends, talking on the phone, or checking your social media at nine o'clock. Be ready to start your work on time.
- Don't ride other people's privileges. You may see people in your office who have permission to come in at fluctuating times based on their jobs and employee deals, but you need to be clear on what your contract states for your position.

- Don't get into a habit of not taking your lunch break or working through lunchtime from your desk.
- If you have a set time for lunch, take it daily. It will add balance to your day and can improve your mental health.
- If you work in an area that is conducive for leaving the office, go out to your car, go for a walk, or go to a store and walk around.
- Do something to break up your day. When you take a moment to reset your brain, get off of your computer, and move away from your tasks, you will be more productive when you get back to work.
- If you do not take your break, people might assume that you do not want one—and they will let you work through lunch every day. There are certain companies that will give you a written warning if you don't take your lunch because legally, you're supposed to, and they could be fined if you don't. If you work in an industry where lunch is occasionally a "working lunch," which means that there's so much work that the company will buy your lunch so that you don't have to take a full break, make sure that you're eating and taking a stretch break during this time.
- Unless you are working on a project that has an exceptional timeline to it, make sure that you stay in the habit of leaving your workplace at the time you are scheduled to leave. If you're off at six-thirty, unless there's something that the team needs to work late on, make sure that you're leaving at six-thirty.

A lot of young professionals believe that working overtime every day shows how dedicated you are, and on occasion, that can be seen as true. However, when you're always working late to do the work that you are expected to complete within the hours that you are required to work, it can send a signal that you cannot keep up and/or meet timelines and due dates.

If you find yourself needing to work overtime on something that is not a special project, stop to assess what's going on. It could be that you're not managing your time effectively because you don't understand a process in the workflow—or there is not enough time allotted for the project.

If you are having trouble completing your work on time, talk to your manager to review the process to make sure that you are in step.

Sometimes, after a careful reassessment, managers realize that your job cannot be completed by one person and will bring on additional help or change the due dates. They don't always know that changes are necessary unless someone brings it to their attention.

Tip: Self-management is important. Don't let your manager recognize this as an issue before you do. If you find that you are constantly struggling with managing your time surrounding projects, set a meeting with your manager to discuss solutions. You might need additional training or clarity on the company's process. If the process is outdated, it might need to be adjusted. Bring the conversation forward in an effort to be proactive but not as a complaint. Let it be known that you are looking forward to success for your team and have a couple of questions that pertain to the process.

DAILY DUTIES

Get a really good understanding of your job description, your duties, and the projects you are expected to accomplish monthly, weekly, and daily. If you're given a project that's due in a month, you should have written guidelines for how to accomplish your goals, including the vision, goals, tasks, timelines, and execution plan that your supervisor can review at any time—or someone else can pick up if you get sick and are not able to complete it.

When setting your timeline, make sure that you're checking in with your supervisor as needed so that if, as you are moving forward, there are any adjustments that need to be made, you will know along the way. Many managers have one-on-one meetings with their staff weekly as a touch point to make sure their employees are on track and to answer any questions. Do not assume that they are going to tell you what to do during these meetings. You will give a brief report on what you are doing. It's a great time for them to comment on your work and say, "Oh yeah, this is great" or "Can you change this?" You'll want to have time to make adjustments and make sure that you have their full buy-in of what you are preparing to present as your final project. Be prepared to give written progress reports weekly. I tell my students all the time that the paper is not written for the benefit of the teacher; it is for the benefit of the student. The reports that you prepare are really preparing you and keeping your thoughts organized.

Tip: Keep your files and records organized. Always remember that your work computer, email, accounts, and office are not yours. They belong to the company, and you should assume that they can or will be reviewed at any time. Consider them public files that will be attached to the reputation of your brand after you leave.

Never store your personal files on your computer. They become the property of the company and are traceable the moment you save them. They also show records of what you are doing with the company's resources. Do not send personal emails from your office account. Keep your files organized. Emergencies happen and if an employee gets sick, has a car accident, or has a baby earlier than anticipated, the truth comes out about their true work style. People should always be able to pick up where you left off.

There was a time when an employee had an emergency and could not come back to work. When looking at their file cabinets, we were shocked that although they had been functioning on the surface level due to their made-up structure, they literally had no files. There were no files in the cabinets; there were just copies of documents stacked on top of each other. It was astonishing and a lot of work to get things in order for their replacement. No one expects an emergency to happen, and the likelihood of you facing something that you never come back from is slim. Keep things prepared for yourself and your team.

Make sure you know who your supervisor and the second person in command is at all times. You may have a specific executive that you report to, but if they're not there, who has the authority and knowledge to make executive decisions on your project? What are the protocols?

Learn what each role on your team does. Who does what—and how does it apply to your job and the success of the team? Understand their job so that you can be a better partner for them and help them accomplish their goals, and then you'll understand how they can help you accomplish your goals based on what they're doing.

Set a daily agenda and create clear daily goals. At the end of each day, set goals for the next day. In the mornings, after checking in with your team to make sure there have been no updates, confirm your agenda for the day. If you complete all your tasks, don't wait for the work to come to you. Talk to your point person about what next steps can be taken.

When you attend video meetings and conferences, bring your full presence. You cannot show up to a meeting in the office and not bring your presence to the meeting. Every time you attend a video meeting, your camera should be on. You should be alert and ready to work. You may have the luxury of not having to be in the room, but your presence and energy are still required.

Tip: Always keep a notepad. When you're new, always keep a small notebook, a tablet, or your phone in your hand—even if you're just meeting with your supervisor for an impromptu five-minute chat. This will enable you to write down what they're saying and get clarity. If you have a question later, you can go back to them and refer to your notes. "I know you said we were going to do numbers one through ten, but I have a question about number five. Will you please clarify?" This lets them know that you are really tuned in, and it helps you stay aligned with their vision.

Ask appropriate questions. Although there are no unintelligent questions, there are questions that are inappropriately positioned in time. Maximize the time you have for conversations with others by asking for answers that you cannot easily find elsewhere. Most people will want to share as much information as they can with you, but nobody wants to have to spoon-feed you from a plate that is right in front of you. People do not want to feel like they have to think or research for you.

Meet all due dates and timelines. Always get clarity from your manager or executive from the beginning of an assignment about when a task or project is due and the timelines that are associated with anything you're working on.

Check in with your supervisor. Until you get into a really great rhythm with your supervisor—where you know how much communication they require as it pertains to your whereabouts—even when you head out to lunch, as a courtesy, let them know. People might not be paying attention to whether you are at your workstation until they need you. If every time they require your support, you are not around, it can be frustrating. If you communicate and say, "Hey, I'm going to head out lunch right now," "Anything else you need before I leave for the day?" "I just got in, and I'll be working on this project—but let me know if you need anything," it gives your managers touch points that are not overwhelming. It lets them know you're on track, available, or not available if they are looking for you.

Don't forget that working is an opportunity and not an obligation that provides you with:

- one-of-a-kind, hands-on learning experiences
- insights into business structure
- exposure to industry practices and company workflow
- real work experience for your resume and bio

KEY TAKEAWAYS

My key takeaways from this section that I will move into action right now are:

_____

_____

_____

_____

_____

_____

_____

_____

_____

_____

_____

_____

_____

_____

_____

_____

_____

_____

_____

_____

_____

PART VII

THE TRUTH BEHIND THE INTERVIEW PROCESS

THE PURPOSE

An interview is a psychological exercise to help interviewers learn more about your personal character, behavior, viewpoints, desires, requirements. and more. Prepare to discuss more than what the interviewer has already reviewed on your resume.

QUICK TIPS TO REMEMBER

TURN YOUR INTERVIEW INTO A MEETING

Executives don't interview for the positions they are considering stepping into. They have meetings of the mind with company decision makers. A meeting of the mind is a meeting to gain an understanding or mutual agreement between two or more parties. After much research, they come confidently to the table with their thoughts and questions about the position. They understand that the opportunity might be a good fit for both parties or that it might not actually be a good fit. Either way, their connection during the meeting could be a win in the long run. You never know if you are going into a meeting to plant the seed of who you are into the minds of those who you may eventually work with in some capacity. You might be going in to pick the harvest you planned to get. Either way can be a win. Show up and represent your brand at a level of excellence.

DRESS FOR THE POSITION YOU WANT

During an interview, people want to be able to envision you in the position you are applying for. Dressing the part is more important than what you look like. It has more to do with signifying that you understand the position and are comfortable with the company culture, that you'll know how to dress for company meetings and outings, and that you will not be uncomfortable in the office setting. The less someone has to teach you, the easier it will be for them to envision you as a natural walking into the position. People want to hire those who are as ready as possible for the position they're looking to fill. If you have an upcoming interview and do not know anyone who works at the company, research what people in your industry wear to work on a regular basis. If it varies in your industry, be bold and call and ask what the company dress code is. Make sure you wear what makes you as comfortable as possible so that you are not fidgeting with your clothes or thinking about your feet hurting based on your shoe selection.

ANALYZE THE POINT OF EACH QUESTION YOU'RE ASKED AND PROVIDE SOLUTION-BASED RESPONSES WHEN POSSIBLE

Before answering any question, ask yourself, "Why would they ask me that question in relation to this particular job?" Since your answers are often used to determine facts about your instincts and personality, be wise about the answers you provide.

PREPARE TO DISCUSS SALARY REQUIREMENTS, UNDERSTANDING THAT STRATEGY IS IMPORTANT

Don't be afraid to talk about money. Be educated on how the standards surrounding your prospective position, industry, education, and experience play into your abilities to negotiate.

JOKES, POLITICS, AND RELIGIOUS CONVERSATIONS ARE NOT APPROPRIATE

Feel free to let people know if there are certain topics outside of work that you prefer not to talk about. You can say, "That is a topic I would prefer to stay away from" or "I have no words." You can say this in a very, friendly, and even lighthearted kind of way.

WRITE REFERENCE NOTES

Write notes after every interview that you can refer to, especially if you are meeting with multiple companies and/or departments. They will help you when you are:

- carefully considering the opportunity
- preparing for the next interview at the same company
- following up with a personalized thank-you card

CONFIRM YOUR FOLLOW-UP CONTACT, TIME FRAME, AND POSSIBLE NEXT STEP

Before you leave the interview, make sure you understand your follow-up procedure. Who should you follow up with and when? Oftentimes, the person you met with will not be the person you will be speaking to about your next steps. Be sure to ask when the company is looking to fill the position. Some companies interview six months before they plan to fill the position. They may know that someone is leaving in six months and are preparing for the transition, or they may be creating a new position that will not be set up for six months. It's your responsibility to inquire about this information so that you can plan and build your strategy accordingly.

FREQUENTLY ASKED QUESTIONS

There are a number of questions that are frequently asked during interviews. Review these twenty questions and be able to answer them with ease. There is more to each question than what appears on the surface. Figure out why they are asking you the question.

1. Why are you interested in this position? This question is asked to identify that you are very familiar with the position and have a very specific interest in it. When you take a job, you are building a relationship with the company. In regular relationships, people want to be around people who understand them, have a very specific interest in them, and are looking to grow with them based on who they are. The same mindset applies to jobs. The company wants to make sure you want to be in relationship with them because you're fully invested, based on who you both are and what you can add to that team. Therefore, when asked this question, briefly reiterate what the position is, does, and is set to do—and how your background makes you a perfect fit.

2. What attracted you to this company? The same mindset applies here. People want to know that you are very familiar with their company. Oftentimes, especially when speaking with young professionals who are interviewing with many companies at one time, the answer comes across as very generic. When they ask what attracted you to their company, it is an opportunity to talk about the specifics of that company, including how they function, their placement in the market, what you've seen them do, what you've read about their plans, and how you want to be involved in what's happening.

3. What can you add to our team? People consider what they want and invest in what they need. Be sure to understand where there's a need for you since it can make the process easier. Company

representatives want to know what you know about them and that you have a unique ability to connect with their team.

    a.   Be sure to research who they already have in position and what they do. You cannot suggest what you can add unless you know what they already have in place and what they might have a need for. Know who the executives and managers are, learn more about their backgrounds, and find out what they add to the team. Perhaps you can share how you might align well with their vision. Go to the business's social media sites to do research and learn more.

    b.   Look for articles about future projects so that you can speak to specifics.

    c.   Speak to at least one thing that differentiates you or would add a bonus or spark to the team and the work they are already doing. Never assume that you are bringing something they do not already have or have considered. Mention how you may serve as a great addition. They might ask, "What can you add to our team?" That's your time to focus on what they currently have in place. It could be something as simple as saying, "Based on your company's amazing development department, my skill set in research could serve as a great asset for developing what you're looking to do next."

4.   How would you like to grow within the company? Based on your career road map and assessments, you should be able to identify how you would like to grow within the company you are interviewing with. Be very clear about how you express your desire to grow because what you say will usually be noted and taken seriously. Interviewers are trying to figure out where you're looking to go and if you're going to be a good fit for their open position. Some people are looking to change their team, and what you say concerning how you'd like to grow might be a great fit for what they want to do next. This is one of the reasons it is important to stay true to brand because you don't know what opportunities might appear. If you're transparent about your long-term goals, you have a better chance of meeting those goals and being placed in those positions.

Tip: When talking about how you would like to advance within the company, be sure to bring the conversation back to express how the position you are being considered for can help you grow toward your goals.

5. How long do you see yourself working in this position before transitioning to your next one? The key to answering this question is understanding how long it might actually take to get acclimated to the position you're applying for. When I'm looking for an assistant, I always ask, "How long can you see yourself working in this position before transitioning to your next level?" If they tell me one year, then it might be hard for me to hire them because I know—with the projects we have in development—it might take them one year to get into a good rhythm with everything that's happening within the organization. If they tell me two years, that works better for me, but every organization has its own needs. You need to be able to identify how long you foresee being able to work in the position you are applying for and what answer you will provide based on your goals and their needs. There might be circumstances that make you change your mind later, but it's good to have a good sense of your plans going in.

6. Can you tell me a little bit about yourself? When people ask you to tell them a little bit about who you are, start by sharing who you are as a professional and as a leader, the business organizations you are affiliated with, and so on. If there is time, and they open the door and ask more about your personal life, which they often will because people have a desire to work with well-balanced people, share surface-level personal information, such as what nonprofits or service work you do, general information on how you like to travel (if that's true), and other activities that bring you joy. Allow them to experience a more personal side of you—but do not get too personal or distract them from who you are as a candidate.

7. What are your strengths and weaknesses? Once you've identified what you want to share as your strengths and weaknesses, you have to connect what you've written down to the position you're applying for. They are looking to find out what strengths and

weaknesses you have that could add to or prevent you from being successful in the position.

8. What really motivates and drives you toward success? This question has to do with your personal mission, why you have the vision for the work you want to do, what drives you past your problems, and what motivates you toward success. What about this job is going to be so aligned with your mission that your mission will naturally drive you toward success?

9. What was your most challenging team experience? Take the time to identify a case scenario. Consider a challenging team experience where you are able to discuss how you and your team came through the issue with some form of success at the end. This may require that you have the ability to identify good in difficult situations. You may discuss:

- the difficulty you faced but identify how you were able to make it through successfully by doing_____.
- although your project was not a complete success, you were successful at learning_____.

10. What would your former supervisor like you to improve? Think back to your last position and consider sharing something that you were encouraged to improve, are actively working on, and will not prevent you from getting the job you are applying for.

Tip: If you know that you need to improve something that is detrimental to your success in your prospective position, determine if there is a way you can get up to speed quickly or consider not taking the job yet. You want to be a successful asset and great professional partner to your team. Make sure you move with integrity and maintain an excellent reputation.

11. Tell me how other people describe you. Don't be shy. The point is to know yourself, develop intentionally, and be aware of how you are perceived by others. It's always great to share that you are sweet and funny, but lead with adjectives that let people in on what it's

like to work with you as a professional, any leadership skills you have, and things that express your personality.

12. What would you like me to know about you? Share something about yourself that is a unique quality about who you are or experience you have that makes you a great fit for the position.

13. What is your starting salary requirement? Before you go in for an interview, always research the standard salary for the position you're applying for, specifically in your industry. After you know the starting salary requirement, you can determine whether you should ask for additional money based on your education and any experience you may be bringing to the company. If the salary for the position you're applying for starts at $65,000, but you've been doing the job for five years and have acquired an exceptional level of expertise, you may ask for $70,000 or negotiate for other benefits. Understand that negotiations are risky, will not always work in your favor, and require a lot of consideration. If you have no experience, you may want to stay at the base rate they are offering if you are interested in the job. You can always ask if there is room for growth down the line.

Tip: Different industries may pay different salaries for the same job—so make sure you have as much information as possible before your interview.

14. What can you tell me about your worst experience with a supervisor, or someone you reported to in any capacity, and how did you cope with the situation? This is a question to reveal how you deal with authority and leadership in challenging times. Provide an honest answer that reveals how you deal with conflict. Remember that how you talk about others is how people will assume you will talk about them. This is not the time to bad-mouth an old supervisor or professor. It is a time to exhibit your ability to deal with conflict.

15. Why do you want to leave your current job? Don't talk about how your boss is difficult. Don't talk about how you can't get along with other employees. Don't bad-mouth your company. Instead, focus on the positives that a transition will bring. Discuss what you want to achieve, how you want to grow, and what you want to

learn. Explain passionately how a move will be great for you and for your new company.

16. Why are you the best candidate for this position? What differentiates you? Describe the incredible passion, desire, and commitment you have for the work outlined in the position that you are applying for. Mention any technical skills or experiences you could bring to the table.

17. Tell me about the toughest decision you had to make in the past six months. This question is being asked to evaluate your ability to solve problems and make great decisions during difficult times.

   ▪ Do you have great judgment and critical decision-making skills?
   ▪ Do you have the ability to see and consider all sides of a problem for all people involved?
   ▪ Do you fold under pressure?
   ▪ Like most people, you have probably experienced some type of drama, and if you have no story to share, even beyond six months, it might be assumed that your experiences have not prepared you for dealing with problems in the workforce or that you don't acknowledge the realities of life around you.

18. What is your leadership style? Managers need to know how they can position you and if you will adapt to their team. While listening to your answer, they will consider the dynamics of their current team while examining if you are someone who needs to have your hands on everything and lead by an authoritative style or if you delegate by nature and assign and trust others to carry out the work at hand. They will also be listening to hear if you are someone who participates with your team, serves as a coach, or has a combination of styles depending on the need. Be prepared to share examples of times when you were called to lead at work or nonwork scenarios. From your answer, they will make their own assessment.

19. What can we expect from you in your first three months? The answer to this question is contingent on the job you are considering, but in

general, it has to do with how you foresee adapting to your position within the first ninety days and positioning yourself for future success. In some companies, the first three months are considered a probationary or grace period. You might answer that you will be getting into a great rhythm with your job, setting your strategic plans for the next twelve months, and getting familiar with the team, but it will depend on the job, company, and industry.

20. What questions do you have for me? Ask questions that will help you determine whether the position will be a great fit for you and demonstrate that you are an incredible candidate.

BONUS QUESTIONS TO ASK

- What do you expect me to accomplish in the first ninety days? This question lets your interviewer know that you are someone who considers the details before making decisions. It also implies that you understand and respect timelines and due dates. It demonstrates that you are aware that there are definite expectations and want to make sure you can meet them in advance. It shows that you have a strategic mindset.

- What are the three traits your top performers have in common? It's presumed that a company's top employees have risen to where they are in part based on their traits that have been proven to work best in their environment. This question is asked to gain an understanding of the behaviors or personalities that work best in this space. Are they creative? Do they work long hours? Are they completely data-driven employees? Most people ask this question to gauge how they will fit into the mix.

- What *really* drives results in this job? This question is asking the interviewer what the heart of the job is. If you work at a retail store, the end goal is to sell products. What really drives the results in the job as a salesperson, however, is your ability to connect with the customer quickly at a level that will encourage them to trust that they should buy into your recommendations. It's important to know what drives the company's results forward so that you'll know if you're able to do what's required before you accept an offer.

- What are the company's highest-priority goals this year—and how would my role contribute? This question lets the interviewer know you are looking at the business side of the company and want to be connected to its productivity and success at a higher level. It expresses that you are not just looking to secure a job and that you want to have an impact with your work.

TYPES OF INTERVIEWS

There are six types of interviews to be aware of. Not all companies put all six into practice, but make sure you are familiar with all of them.

THE SCREENING INTERVIEW (PREQUALIFICATION PROCESS)

- The first point of contact determines whether you will receive an invitation to move forward in the process. Most people don't consider the initial call or email you receive to be an official interview, but it is. From the moment someone makes contact with you in response to a job you have applied for, the interview process begins. What you say during this call, video chat, or email exchange establishes whether you will get an invitation to another interview. Everything from that moment on is being observed.
- How long it takes you to respond: When you are in an interview season, make a habit of checking your voice mails and emails every few hours during the day, especially around four o'clock, to ensure that if you missed a message, there is enough time to respond and possibly receive a callback before the end of the day. You should never take longer than twenty-four hours to respond to a recruiter. You never know what phase of interviewing the company you're applying to is in. Although your resume is holding your place in line, so to speak, there are usually other people in line with you. The company may be desperate to fill the position. Sometimes,

whoever calls the recruiter back first gets the next interview slot. You don't want to miss a job opportunity because you were not managing your messages appropriately.

- Show excitement and connection to the opportunity.
- People want to know that you really want to work with them and that you didn't randomly apply to their company just because you needed a job.
- Always know, from the start of the conversation, which company's representative you're talking to and the position they are calling you about. If you've applied to several companies and answer a call from a recruiter, confirm their name and the company they are calling from in the first three seconds. Do not try to see if you can identify who they are along the way because if you do you won't be completely tuned in to the call because you'll be trying to figure out which position they are referring to.
- You can ask about the company, but you are expected to know which position it relates to. If you applied to two positions at the same company, clarify which one they are making reference to during your call.
- Keep a job list on your phone. Every time you apply for a job, list the company name, the position, the date, and any relevant details that you want to remember for your interview and consideration process. This will give you a quick reference sheet for your phone interviews.
- Be aware of your tone and be confident in your responses.
- Make yourself memorable.
- Try to come across as attentive and eager to discuss the possibilities.
- Your confidence level should be at a ten, based on the time you have invested in your personal development and the knowledge you obtained during your research of the company and position.
- The person who is calling should find your personality refreshing.
- Many recruiters have called at least twenty people before they called you. Be memorable and make them want to meet with you. Don't be over the top but be genuinely excited.
- Be aware of how you handle the offer to discuss your thoughts on the possibilities ahead.

Tip: As soon as you answer a recruiter's call, your screening interview starts. You have officially joined the meeting. If you are applying to multiple positions, keep your job list on you at all times so that you're always prepared to have a discussion about your thoughts. If you're at a restaurant or another loud venue, it's better to let it go to voice mail and quickly go someplace quiet, grab your notes, and call them right back so that you can be collected and focused on the interview.

Some recruiters might ask you about your history and resume over the phone, but most will reserve these conversations for your one-on-one in-person or video meeting. However, if they are in a rush to fill the position, they may be looking to accelerate the process by narrowing down candidates during the first call. Be prepared.

THE ONE-ON-ONE INTERVIEW (FIT TEST)

- This puts a face and a story to the resume. This is the time when people want to meet you and experience how you carry yourself. They also want to hear the story behind your resume and your plans for the future.
- Understand that you don't arrive when you enter the office. You arrive when you enter the neighborhood. People are watching and will remember if they saw you or witnessed a kind gesture you showed someone at a coffee shop or if you weren't so kind. You never know who will see you driving down the street, getting off of the bus, or sitting in the parking lot. Make sure that you are not on your phone in the elevators, lobby, or bathroom because word travels fast, and those conversations are often reported back by people you didn't know worked at the company you were meeting with.
- Video meetings: Always expect to show up ready for a camera. For virtual meetings: your video, lighting, and sound—or lack thereof—can have a great effect on your interview. Even though you may not be in the room, it should always feel like you are. Some companies will video tape your in-person interviews to share with their teams later.

- Before you go into this interview, be sure to research and learn as much as you can about the company's history, current status, and future plans. You want to have an educated conversation, ask smart questions, and gain insight for what you were not able to acquire in your research.

- Upgrade your interview to a meeting. Remember to upgrade your interview to a meeting of the minds. Turn it into a great conversation about the possibilities ahead. This is an opportunity to meet and network with the company representative and for them to meet and network with you. Make it memorable and a moment they will want to share in five years about how they had the pleasure of meeting you when you applied for a position at their company. Since you are both in the same industry, you will probably see each other in the future—regardless of what happens in this interview. You might interview for a job and not get it, but based on the impression you leave with the company representative about who you are as a professional, you may get a call for a different position in the future for something they thought you might want and be a good fit for.

THE SECOND INTERVIEW (THE RETAKE)

- When you are asked to come back for a second interview, it is often because they are interested in who you are, have narrowed down their selection to a few candidates, and would like to have a deeper conversation comparing your skill sets and traits to the other applicants.
- This is when you should reiterate why you are the best fit based on your experience, skill set, and awareness of the company's culture.
- This is an opportunity to ask clarifying questions that you were not able to ask before about day-to-day job duties, benefits, and team structure.

PEER INTERVIEWS (TEAM MEMBERS)

Peer interviews are interviews between candidates and their potential peers. If you get invited to a peer interview, although it is not a guarantee for the job, it usually means that they are seriously considering you for the position. This helps the team determine whether they'd be comfortable with you as the new hire.

The team may have similar questions to the ones we addressed earlier. They may have questions that are closely related to what their department does on a day-to-day basis. They might ask, "How do you foresee adding value to our particular team?" The following are questions you can ask the team:

- What makes your team blend well?
- What is your team's most successful accomplishment to date?
- What does the future look like for this team?

PANEL INTERVIEWS (GROUP)

Panel interviews are when two or more people interview someone at the same time. Company executives, managers, team members, and human resources representatives may be invited in to ask questions. Preparation is key.

- Find out who will be on the panel. When you receive the invitation to join a panel interview or group meeting, boldly ask who will be in attendance. This will allow you to do your research. Most people will tell you if you inquire. Once you have the list, look up the company representatives on the company's website, social media sites, and the internet to learn more about their jobs, personal missions, and personalities. Building a quick connection with those on the panel requires some understanding of who they are. Looking them up will help you identify who they are. Articles they have written or been interviewed in may provide you with insights about where they are looking to go within your industry, which may help you during the interview.

- Study the company as a whole. Learn more about the direction they are going in and what has happened recently. They may ask you how you would add to the success of one of their current projects or do something differently. Even if you're applying for an entry-level assistant position, your answer to that question should still be meaningful and show value. If that were the case, you might say, "I understand that my assistance to the CEO will provide support, organization, and ease that will ultimately have an effect on the company's operational flow."

- Bring your full professional presence into the room. This is a great example of utilizing confidence and humility. Be confident enough to share your thoughts and humble enough to answer questions openly. Use your body language to reflect your confidence.

- Make your interview conversational. Read the room and engage with everyone. From the time you walk into the room—and through every answer you provide—comfortably address everyone in the room. Although you may initially begin by addressing the person who asks a question, bring everyone into your answer by intentionally glancing at others while speaking. Make eye contact and use gestures that reflect a confident and balanced personality.

- Prepare a brief introduction and set the tone for what they should expect. You will probably be formally introduced by the person who set up the interview, but you should still be prepared to address the room in a sentence or two before things officially start. For example, after being introduced, you might say, "Good morning. Thank you all for taking the time to meet with me this morning to discuss the _____position. I am looking forward to our conversation today."

- Ask smart questions. Don't forget that interviews are a part of a psychological analysis. When preparing your questions, remember that intent is a key factor. Ask questions that reflect that you're wise enough to know which questions to ask. It's like math. Most people are not going to ask questions about multiplication if they don't understand addition. Ask questions that reflect your level of understanding.

- Bring a copy of your resume for each person on the panel. Although it may not be necessary, it provides them with a sheet for notes that already has your information on the back. Some recruiters will tell you in advance if you need to bring one for others—but always bring one for yourself.

- Even though you may need to refer to your resume to reference a date before the interview starts, it sends a terrible sign that you have not been engaged in your own life enough to remember it if you have to refer to your resume to recall what you've done.

- Take great notes. They can help you circle back to a point someone makes that you want to address after they finish talking. This can also be beneficial after your interview as a point of reference.

- Build rapport and try to make strong connections. Every interview is a networking opportunity and a commercial, so to speak, where you get to share sound bites of who you are with others and learn more about the people on the panel, their positions, and the company. Remember that they are professionals in your industry that you may work with later.

LUNCH OR DINNER INTERVIEWS (SOCIAL TEST)

This interview takes place at a restaurant to further discuss a candidate's qualifications and assess their social, communication, and people skills.

- Company representatives want to observe your social presence to detect if it will be a mirror of their image when you are out as one of their representatives. Be polite to everyone, friendly, and personable. When it is time to discuss business, be focused.

- Be prepared to answer any final questions and reiterate your qualifications to the company representative.

- Arrive early. Allow your interviewer to feel as though they are walking right into the interview as soon as they arrive. Being early will reflect your time-management abilities. When you are late, you're not focused. If you can, drive to the location in advance so that you are familiar with the area and the parking options. Do whatever will make you comfortable. I always check out the menu in advance so that I am not spending five minutes trying to figure out what I want to eat.

- Order light food and no alcohol. When you are invited to the best restaurant, it can be hard to remember that your invitation is not about the food.
- Don't get caught up in where you are—and remember why you are there.
- Make sure you order light food. Avoid anything that will make you sleepy or make you slouch.
- Don't stuff yourself—even if the food is delicious. Eat enough to be social, but don't let the food get in the way of the meeting.
- If possible, order something that is not messy, will allow you to talk, doesn't require that you use your hands, can be cut into bite-sized pieces, and won't stick to your teeth.
- It's always best to avoid ordering alcohol because it can come across as unprofessional and can be a test to see if you would order alcohol on a regular basis when out at work meetings. Sometimes you might be sitting with an executive who is drinking and insists that you order a drink to see whether or not you would keep it professional.
- Turn off or silence your phone.

AFTER EVERY INTERVIEW

WRITE NOTES

SEND THANK-YOU NOTES

FOLLOW UP WITH YOUR CONTACT

POST INTERVIEW TO-DOS

- As soon as you leave any interview, write down any notes that will help you remember important facts about what was said or instructions you may have been given.
- Send thank-you cards. If you can, buy a box of plain thank-you cards from the discount store and a roll of stamps from the post office. As soon as you come out of an interview, mail a handwritten thank-you card to the person or people you met with and thank them for the opportunity. If you are unable to buy physical cards, you can use digital cards if you have the person's email address.
- Before you leave, confirm the company's next steps in their hiring process, when you should expect to hear something back, or if and when you should follow up and with whom.

KEY TAKEAWAYS

My key takeaways from this section that I will move into action right now are:

_____

_____

_____

_____

_____

_____

_____

_____

_____

_____

_____

_____

_____

_____

_____

_____

_____

_____

_____

_____

_____

_____

NEXT STEPS

Congratulations! You have made it through our coaching session, started developing your professional syllabus based on the goals you plan to graduate into, have begun to develop the standards for your professional scripts, and have begun building your process. You are ready to begin putting everything into practice for your next level.

Always remember the keys to brand development that are listed in the chart below. They will serve as a guideline for your ongoing advancement.

You'll continue to discover new things about your brand, and you'll need to set your expectations accordingly. After you have developed your brand name, you'll grow and rebrand along the way. Keep looking and preparing for opportunities of growth and service and moving forward on your career road map. Remember that the journey is one of the most exciting parts of the trip, especially when you have prepared and packed what you'll need. Keep networking with purpose and intent, form partnerships with strategy in mind, and stay savvy at every level of your growth. Be sure to keep your social media channels properly aligned with programming that is fitting for your life's plans. Develop organization affiliations that will help you grow, provide you with a place to serve, and give you a place to exercise the language of your business.

10 KEYS TO BRAND DEVELOPMENT

DISCOVER YOUR BRAND	SET YOUR EXPECTATIONS	DEVELOP YOUR BRAND NAME	PREPARE FOR FUTURE OPPORTUNITIES	CREATE CAREER ROAD MAPS
NETWORK EFFECTIVELY	FORM STRATEGIC PARTNERSHIPS	BECOME BUSINESS SAVVY	LAUNCH YOUR BRAND ON SOCIAL MEDIA SUCCESSFULLY	DEVELOP ORGANIZATIONS AFFILIATIONS

MOMENTS OF FOCUS LLC

Intern to VP ® is the property of Moments of Focus LLC © All Rights Reserved DO NOT DUPLICATE

Additional things to remember:

- Your professional syllabus should:
  - be based on what you want to graduate into next
  - be structured on the experience and knowledge you need to graduate
  - be centered around the who, what, when, and where you can gain credits
  - include a timeline and scheduled opportunities
- Continue to develop sound bites or commercials about who you are through your professional scripts, which represent the actual episodes you're producing for your life.
- Every time you create an action plan, make sure it has what it needs to move into the next stage of development.

It has been a joy to add to this part of your journey. I am looking forward to the greatness you add to the world based on all the seeds you have planted in this work.

ACKNOWLEDGMENTS

I must thank God for giving me the vison, ability, and opportunity to help other people multiply their gifts, turn on their lights, and flourish in their visions.

Thank you, Alani, for your kind words, encouragement, and love — Aaliyah for your ear, love, and support, and DeNoire for your involvement, support, and love. To the rest of my family, friends, and colleagues who supported me along the journey, thank you.

A special thank-you to my corporate, university, organization, and educational partners who have pushed to get this training program and book to their employees, members, and students.

For more information about continuous coaching and training, as well as licensing and partnerships opportunities, contact us through www.momentsoffocus.com.

Intern to VP* is the property of Moments of Focus* LLC.

ABOUT THE AUTHOR

BeNeca Ward is a Brand & Leadership Development Expert, Executive Advisor, International Speaker, and Author who was recognized by the White House in 2010 for her leadership abilities. As an executive coach and advisor, she's called upon to help Fortune 100/500 companies, executives, entrepreneurs, professionals, athletes, and young adults develop and take their brands, partnerships, and leadership to the next level.

She's been a featured speaker for the United State of Women Conference, National Football League (NFL) Players Association, 40thAnnual California Hispanic Chambers of Commerce Convention, CA Board of Equalization's Connecting Women to Power Business Conference, and more. She served as an instructor at the Center for Executive Development at UC San Diego's Rady School of Management and was nominated for the Los Angeles Black Business Leaders Hall of Fame. As an author, BeNeca received an NAACP Image Award Nomination and was recognized as a community leader.

Her company Moments of Focus® works with executives who seek expertise to fully develop their business objectives, growth strategies, executive presence, professional management styles, transition plans, and bottom-line results. Companies and universities bring their young professionals and teams through the Moments of Focus® signature programs to help them develop professional brand identities that stand strong, partner well with their organizations, and enhance their visions, values, patterns of thought, and execution.

As someone who began her career in the entertainment business as a high school student and went from intern to becoming Vice President, BeNeca provides countless hours as an advisor for young professionals across the country. She has worked with Junior Achievement, the Fulfilment Fund, California National Guard's Youth Academy, and other organizations, universities across the country, and the Los Angeles Unified School District where she served as the chair for the Young Women's Leadership Community.

Printed in the United States
by Baker & Taylor Publisher Services